P9-CMF-758

Plate I.

From "Sylva Sylvarum," 1627.

Plate I.

FROM "SYLVA SYLVARUM," 1627.

BACON

IS

SHAKE-SPEARE

BY

SIR EDWIN DURNING-LAWRENCE, BART.

B.A., LL.B., ETC.

"Every hollow Idol is dethroned by skill,
insinuation and regular approach."

Together with a Reprint of

Bacon's Promus of Formularies and Elegancies

Collated, with the Original MS. by the late F. B. BICKLEY,
and revised by F. A. HERBERT, of the British Museum.

THE JOHN McBRIDE CO.

NEW YORK

1910

TO THE READER.

THE plays known as Shakespeare's are at the present time universally acknowledged to be the "Greatest birth of time," the grandest production of the human mind. Their author also is generally recognised as the greatest genius of all the ages. The more the marvellous plays are studied, the more wonderful they are seen to be.

Classical scholars are amazed at the prodigious amount of knowledge of classical lore which they display. Lawyers declare that their author must take rank among the greatest of lawyers, and must have been learned not only in the theory of law, but also intimately acquainted with its forensic practice. In like manner, travellers feel certain that the author must have visited the foreign cities and countries which he so minutely and graphically describes.

It is true that at a dark period for English literature certain critics denied the possibility of Bohemia being accurately described as by the sea, and pointed out the "manifest absurdity" of speaking of the "port" at Milan; but a wider knowledge of the actual facts have vindicated the author at the expense of his unfortunate critics. It is the same with respect to other matters referred to in the plays. The expert possessing special knowledge of any subject invariably discovers that the plays shew that their author was well acquainted with almost all that was known at the time about that particular subject.

And the knowledge is so extensive and so varied that it is not too much to say that there is not a single living man capable of perceiving half of the learning involved in the production of the plays. One of the greatest students of law publicly declared, while he was editor of the *Law Times*, that although he thought that he knew something of law, yet he was not ashamed to confess that he had not sufficient legal knowledge or mental capacity to enable him to fully comprehend a quarter of the law contained in the plays.

Of course, men of small learning, who know very little of classics and still less of law, do not experience any of these difficulties, because they are not able to perceive how great is the vast store of learning exhibited in the plays.

There is also shewn in the plays the most

perfect knowledge of Court etiquette, and of the manners and the methods of the greatest in the land, a knowledge which none but a courtier moving in the highest circles could by any possibility have acquired.

In his diary, Wolfe Tone records that the French soldiers who invaded Ireland behaved exactly like the French soldiers are described as conducting themselves at Agincourt in the play of "Henry V," and he exclaims, "It is marvellous!" (Wolfe Tone also adds that Shakespeare could never have seen a French soldier, but we know that Bacon while in Paris had had considerable experience of them.)

The mighty author of the immortal plays was gifted with the most brilliant genius ever conferred upon man. He possessed an intimate and accurate acquaintance, which could not have been artificially acquired, with all the intricacies and mysteries of Court life. He had by study obtained nearly all the learning that could be gained from books. And he had by travel and experience acquired a knowledge of cities and of men that has never been surpassed.

Who was in existence at that period who could by any possibility be supposed to be this universal genius? In the days of Queen Elizabeth, for the first time in human history, one such man appeared, the man who is described as the marvel and mystery of the age, and this was the man known to us under the name of Francis Bacon.

In answer to the demand for a "mechanical proof that Bacon is Shakespeare" I have added a chapter shewing the meaning of "Honorificabilitudinitatibus," and I have in Chapter XIV. shewn how completely the documents recently discovered by Dr. Wallace confirm the statements which I had made in the previous chapters.

I have also annexed a reprint of Bacon's "Promus," which has recently been collated with the original manuscript. "Promus" signifies Storehouse, and the collection of "Fourmes and Elegancyes" stored therein was largely used by Bacon in the Shakespeare plays, in his own acknowledged works, and also in some other works for which he was mainly responsible.

I trust that students will derive considerable pleasure and profit from examining the "Promus" and from comparing the words and phrases, as they are there preserved, with the very greatly extended form in which many of them finally appeared.

EDWIN DURNING-LAWRENCE.

CONTENTS.

LIST OF ILLUSTRATIONS.

The Ornamental Headings of the various Chapters are mostly variations of the "Double A" ornament found in certain Shakespeare Quarto Plays, and in various other books published *circa* 1590-1650.

A few references will be found below:—

Title Page, and *To the Reader*.

Shakespeare's Works. 1623.

Contents. Page ix.

North's "Lives." 1595.
Spenser's "Faerie Queene." 1609, 1611.
Works of King James. 1616.
Purchas' "Pilgrimages." 1617.
Bacon's "Novum Organum." 1620.
Seneca's Works. 1620.
Speed's "Great Britaine." 1623.
Bacon's "Operum Moralium." 1638.

Plate II.

Portrait of Francis Bacon. By Van Somer.
Engraved by W. C. Edwards.

Plate II.

Portrait of Francis Bacon. By Van Somer.
Engraved by W. C. Edwards.

Bacon is Shakespeare.

CHAPTER I.

"What does it matter whether the immortal works were written by Shakespeare (of Stratford) or by another man who bore (or assumed) the same name?"

SOME twenty years ago, when this question was first propounded, it was deemed an excellent joke, and I find that there still are a great number of persons who seem unable to perceive that the question is one of considerable importance.

When the Shakespeare revival came, about eighty or ninety years ago, people said "pretty well for Shakespeare" and the "learned" men of that period were rather ashamed that Shakespeare should be deemed to be "*the*" English poet.

"Three poets in three distant ages born,
"Greece, Italy and England did adorn,
. . . .
"The force of Nature could no further go,
"To make a third she joined the other two."

Dryden did not write these lines in reference to Shakespeare but to Milton. Where will you find the person who to-day thinks Milton comes within any measurable distance of the greatest genius among the sons of earth who was called by the name of Shakespeare?

Ninety-two years ago, viz.: in June 1818, an article appeared in *Blackwood's Edinburgh Magazine*, under the heading "Time's Magic Lantern. No. V. Dialogue between Lord Bacon and Shakspeare" [Shakespeare being spelled Shakspeare]. The dialogue speaks of "Lord" Bacon and refers to him as being engaged in transcribing the "Novum Organum" when Shakspeare enters with a letter from Her Majesty (meaning Queen Elizabeth) asking him, Shakspeare, to see "her own" sonnets now in the keeping of *her* Lord Chancellor.

Of course this is all topsy turvydom, for in Queen Elizabeth's reign Bacon was never "Lord" Bacon or Lord Chancellor.

But to continue, Shakspeare tells Bacon "Near to Castalia there bubbles also a fountain of petrifying water, wherein the muses are wont to dip whatever posies have met the approval of Apollo; so that the slender foliage which originally sprung forth in the cherishing brain of a true poet becomes hardened in all its leaves and glitters as if it were carved out of rubies and emeralds. The elements have afterwards no power over it."

Bacon. Such will be the fortune of your own productions.

Shakspeare. Ah my Lord! Do not encourage me to hope so. I am but a poor unlettered man, who seizes whatever rude conceits his own natural vein supplies him with, upon the enforcement of haste and necessity; and therefore I fear that such as are of deeper studies than myself, will find many flaws in my handiwork to laugh at both now and hereafter.

Bacon. He that can make the multitude laugh and weep as you do Mr. Shakspeare need not fear scholars. . . . . More scholarship might have sharpened your judgment but the particulars whereof a character is composed are better assembled by force of imagination than of judgment. . . . . . .

Shakspeare. My Lord thus far I know, that the first glimpse and conception of a character in my mind, is always engendered by chance and accident. We shall suppose, for instance, that I, sitting in a tap-room, or standing in a tennis court. The behaviour of some one fixes my attention. . . . . Thus comes forth Shallow, and Slender, and Mercutio, and Sir Andrew Aguecheek.

Bacon. These are characters who may be found alive in the streets. But how frame you such interlocutors as Brutus and Coriolanus?

Shakspeare. By searching histories, in the first place, my Lord, for the germ. The filling up afterwards comes rather from feeling than observation. I turn myself into a Brutus or a Coriolanus for the time; and can, at least in fancy, partake sufficiently of the nobleness of their nature, to put proper words in their mouths. . . . . .

> My knowledge of the tongues is but small, on which account I have read ancient authors mostly at secondhand. I remember, when I first came to London, and began to be a hanger-on at the theatres, a great desire grew in me for more learning than had fallen to my share at Stratford; but fickleness and impatience, and the bewilderment caused by new objects, dispersed that wish into empty air. . . . . ."

This ridiculous and most absurd nonsense, which appeared in 1818 in *Blackwood's Edinburgh Magazine* was deemed so excellent and so *instructive* that (slightly abridged) it was copied into "Reading lessons for the use of public and private schools" by John Pierpont, of Boston, U.S.A., which was published in London nearly twenty years later, viz., in 1837.

As I said before, the dialogue is really all topsy turvydom, for the writer must have known perfectly well that Bacon was not Lord Keeper till 1617, the year after Shakspeare's death in 1616, and was not made Lord Chancellor till 1618, and that he is not supposed to have began to write the "Novum Organum" before the death of Queen Elizabeth.

I have therefore arrived at the conclusion that the whole article was really intended to poke fun at the generally received notion that the author of the plays was an *un*lettered man, who picked up his knowledge at tavern doors and in taprooms and tennis courts. I would specially refer to the passage where Bacon asks "How frame you such interlocutors as Brutus and Coriolanus?" and Shakspeare replies "By searching histories, in the first place, my Lord, for the germ. The filling up afterwards comes rather from feeling than observation. I turn myself into a Brutus or a Coriolanus for the time and can at least in fancy partake sufficiently of the nobleness of their nature to put proper words in their mouths."

Surely this also must have been penned to open the eyes of the public to the absurdity of the popular conception of the author of the plays as an *un*lettered man who "had small Latin and less Greek"!

The highest scholarship not only in this country and in Germany but throughout the world has been for many years concentrated upon the classical characters portrayed in the plays, and the adverse criticism of former days has given place to a reverential admiration for the marvellous knowledge of antiquity displayed throughout the plays in the presentation of the historical characters of by-gone times; classical authority being found for nearly every word put into their mouths.

What does it matter whether the immortal works were written by Shakspeare (of Stratford) or by a great and learned man who assumed the name Shakespeare to "Shake a lance at Ignorance"? We should not forget that this phrase "Shake a lance at Ignorance" is contemporary, appearing in Ben Jonson's panegyric in the Shakespeare folio of 1623.

CHAPTER II.

The Shackspere Monument, Bust, and Portrait.

In the year 1909 Mr. George Hookham in the January number of the *National Review* sums up practically all that is really known of the life of William Shakspeare of Stratford as follows:—

'We only know that he was born at Stratford, of 'illiterate parents—(we do *not* know that he went 'to school there)—that, when 18½ years old, he 'married Anne Hathaway (who was eight years 'his senior, and who bore him a child six months 'after marriage); that he had in all three children 'by her (whom with their mother he left, and 'went to London, having apparently done his 'best to desert her before marriage);—that in 'London he became an actor with an interest in a 'theatre, and was reputed to be the writer of 'plays;—that he purchased property in Stratford, 'to which town he returned;—engaged in pur-'chases and sales and law-suits (of no biographical 'interest except as indicating his money-making 'and litigious temperament); helped his father in 'an application for coat armour (to be obtained

Plate III.

The Stratford Monument, from Dugdale's Warwickshire, 1656.

Plate III.

THE STRATFORD MONUMENT, FROM DUGDALE'S WARWICKSHIRE, 1656.

Plate IV.

The Stratford Monument as it appears at the present time.

Plate IV.

The Stratford Monument as it appears at the present time.

'by false pretences); promoted the enclosure of 'common lands at Stratford (after being guaran- 'teed against personal loss); made his will—and 'died at the age of 52, without a book in his 'possession, and leaving nothing to his wife but 'his second best bed, and this by an afterthought.

'No record of friendship with anyone more 'cultured than his fellow actors.

'No letter,—only two contemporary reports of 'his conversation, one with regard to the commons 'enclosure as above, and the other in circum- 'stances not to be recited unnecessarily.

'In a word we know his parentage, birth, marriage, 'fatherhood, occupation, his wealth and his chief 'ambition, his will and his death, and absolutely 'nothing else; his death being received with 'unbroken and ominous silence by the literary 'world, not even Ben Jonson who seven years 'later glorified the plays *in excelsis*, expending so 'much as a quatrain on his memory.'

To this statement by Mr. George Hookham I would add that we know W. Shakspeare was christened 26th April 1564, that his Will which commences "In the name of god Amen! I Willim Sha*c*kspeare, of Stratford upon Avon, in the countie of warr gent in perfect health and memorie, god be praysed," was dated 25th (January altered to) March 1616, and it was proved 22nd June 1616, Shakspeare having died 23rd April 1616, four weeks after the date of the Will.

We also know that a monument was erected to

him in Stratford Church. And because L. Digges, in his lines in the Shakespeare folio of 1623 says "When Time dissolves thy Stratford Moniment,"* it is supposed that the monument must have been put up before 1623. But we should remember that as Mrs. Stopes (who is by no means a Baconian) pointed out in the *Monthly Review* of April 1904, the original monument was not like the present monument which shews a man with a pen in his hand; but was the very different monument which will be found depicted in Sir William Dugdale's "Antiquities of Warwickshire," published in 1656. The bust taken from this is shewn on Plate 5, Page 14, and the whole monument on Plate 3, Page 8.

The figure bears no resemblance to the usually accepted likeness of Shakspeare. It hugs a sack of wool, or a pocket of hops to its belly and does not hold a pen in its hand.

In Plate 6, Page 15, is shewn the bust from the monument as it exists at the present time, with the great pen in the right hand and a sheet of paper under the left hand. The whole monument is shewn on Plate 4, Page 9.

The face seems copied from the mask of the so-called portrait in the 1623 folio, which is shewn in Plate 8. It is desirable to look at that picture very carefully, because every student ought to know that the portrait in the title-page of the first folio edition of the plays published in 1623, which was drawn by Martin

* Digges really means "When Time dissolves thy Stratford Mask."

Plate V.

The Stratford Bust, from Dugdale's Warwickshire, published 1656.

Plate V.

THE STRATFORD BUST, FROM DUGDALE'S WARWICKSHIRE, PUBLISHED 1656.

Plate VI.

THE STRATFORD BUST AS IT APPEARS AT THE PRESENT TIME.

Plate VI.

The Stratford Bust as it appears at the present time.

M^R. WILLIAM

SHAKESPEARES

COMEDIES,
HISTORIES, and
TRAGEDIES.

Publiſhed according to the True Originall Copies.

LONDON

Printed by Iſaac Iaggard, and Ed. Blount. 1623.

Plate VII.

FACSIMILE OF TITLE PAGE, REDUCED IN SIZE.

Plate VII.

Facsimile of the Title Page of the first folio edition of the Shakespeare Plays, 1623.

Plate VIII.

Full Size Facsimile of part of the Title Page of the 1623 Shakespeare Folio.

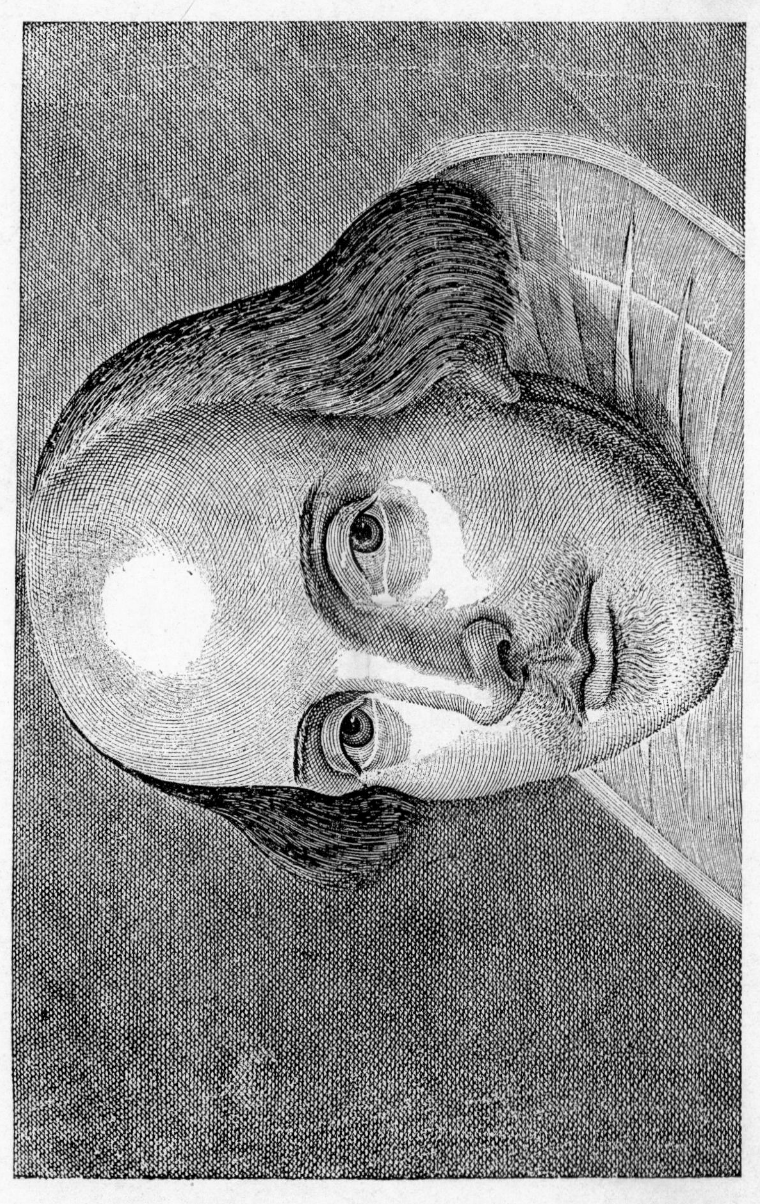

LONDON

Printed by Isaac Iaggard, and Ed. Blount. 1623.

Photo-reproduction, full size from the Title-page of the Shakespeare First Folio.

Plate VIII.

Plate VIII.

Facsimile, Full Size, of the Original Portrait [so-called] of "Shakespeare," from the 1623 Folio.

Droeshout, is cunningly composed of two left arms and a mask. Martin Droeshout, its designer, was, as Mr. Sidney Lee tells us, but 15 years of age when Shakspeare died. He is not likely therefore ever to have seen the actor of Stratford, yet this is the "Authentic," that is the "Authorised" portrait of Shakspeare, although there *is* no question—there *can be* no possible question—that in fact it is a cunningly drawn cryptographic picture, shewing two left arms and a mask.

The back of the left arm which does duty for the right arm is shewn in Plate 10, Page 26. Every tailor will admit that this is not and cannot be the front of the right arm, but is, without possibility of doubt, the back of the left arm.

Plate 11 shews the front of the left arm, and you at once perceive that you are no longer looking at the back of the coat but at the front of the coat.

Now in Plate 12, Page 32, you see the mask. Especially note that the ear is a mask ear and stands out curiously; note also how distinct the line shewing the edge of the mask appears. Perhaps the reader will perceive this more clearly if he turns the page upside down.

Plate 13, Page 33, depicts a real face, that of Sir Nicholas Bacon, eldest son of the Lord Keeper, from a contemporary portrait by Zucchero, lately in the Duke of Fife's Collection. This shews by contrast the difference between the portrait of a living man, and the drawing of a lifeless mask with the double line from ear to chin. Again examine Plates 8, Pages 20, 21, the complete portrait in the folio. The reader having seen the separate portions, will, I trust, be able now to perceive that this portrait is correctly characterised as cunningly composed of two left arms and a mask.

While examining this portrait, the reader should study the lines that describe it in the Shakespeare folio of 1623, a facsimile of which is here inserted.

To the Reader.

This Figure, that thou here seest put,
It was for gentle Shakespeare cut;
Wherein the Grauer had a strife
with Nature, to out-doo the life:
O, could he but haue drawne his wit
As well in brasse, as he hath hit
His face; the Print would then surpasse
All, that was euer writ in brasse.
But, since he cannot, Reader, looke
Not on his Picture, but his Booke.

Plate IX. B. I.

VERSES ASCRIBED TO BEN JONSON, FROM THE 1623 FOLIO EDITION OF SHAKESPEARE'S WORKS.

Plate X.

The Back of the Left Arm, from Plate VIII.

Plate X.

The Back of the Left Arm, from Plate VIII.

Plate XI.

The Front of the Left Arm, from Plate VIII.

Plate XI.

The Front of the Left Arm, from Plate VIII.

"He hath *hit* his face"

It is thought that *hit* means *hid* as in Chaucer's Squiere's Tale, line 512 etc.

"Right as a serpent *hit* him under floures
Til he may seen his tyme for to byte"

If indeed "hit" be intended to be read as "hid" then these ten lines are no longer the cryptic puzzle which they have hitherto been considered to be, but in conjunction with the portrait, they clearly reveal the true facts, that the real author is writing left-handedly, that means secretly, in shadow, with his face hidden behind a mask or pseudonym.

We should also notice "out-doo" is spelled with a hyphen. In the language of to-day and still more in that of the time of Shakespeare all, or nearly all, words beginning with *out* may be read reversed, out-bar is bar out, out-bud is bud out, out-crop is crop out, out-fit is fit out, and so on through the alphabet.

If therefore we may read "out-doo the life" as "doo out the life" meaning "shut out the real face of the living man" we perceive that here also we are told "that the real face is hidden."

The description, with the head line "To the Reader" and the signature "B. I.," forms twelve lines, the words of which can be turned into numerous significant anagrams, etc., to which, however, no allusion is made in the present work. But our readers will find that if all the letters are counted (the two v.v.'s in line nine being counted as four letters) they will amount to the number 287. In subsequent chapters a good deal is said about this number, but here we only desire to say that we are "informed" that the "Great Author" intended to reveal himself 287 years after 1623, the date when the First Folio was published, that is in the present year, 1910, when very numerous tongues will be loosened.

Examine once more the original Stratford Bust, Plate 5, Page 14, and the present Stratford Bust, Plate 6, Page 15, *with the large pen in the right hand.*

If the Stratford actor were indeed the author of the plays it was most appropriate that he should have a pen in his hand. But in the original monument as shewn in Plate 3, Page 8, the figure hugs a sack of wool or a pocket of hops or may be a cushion. For about 120 years, this continued to be the Stratford effigy and shewed nothing that could in any way connect the man portrayed, with literary work. I believe that this was not accidental. I think that everybody in Stratford must have known that William "Sha*ck*speare" could not write so much as his own name, for I assert that we possess nothing which can by any reasonable possibility be deemed to be his signature.

Plate XII.

The [Mask] Head, from the [so-called] Portrait, by Droeshout, in the 1623 Folio.

Plate XII.

The [Mask] Head, from the [so-called] Portrait, by Droeshout, in the 1623 Folio.

Plate XIII.

Sir Nicholas Bacon, from the Painting by Zucchero.

Plate XIII.

Sir Nicholas Bacon, from the Painting by Zucchero.

CHAPTER III.

The so-called "Signatures."

In Plate 14, Page 36, are shewn the five so-called signatures. These five being the only pieces of writing in the world that can, even by the most ardent Stratfordians, be supposed to have been written by Shakspeare's pen; let us consider them carefully. The Will commences "In the name of God Amen I Willim Shackspeare." It is written upon three sheets of paper and each sheet bears a supposed signature. The Will is dated in Latin "Vicesimo quinto die [Januarij] Mtij Anno Regni Dni nri Jacobi, nunc R Anglie, &c. decimo quarto & Scotie xlix° annoq Dni 1616", or shortly in English 25th March 1616.

Shakspeare died 23rd April 1616 just four weeks after publishing his will.

I say after "PUBLISHING his Will" advisedly, for such is the attestation, viz., "Witnes to the publyshing hereof,

"Fra: Collyns
Julius Shawe
John Robinson
Hamnet Sadler
Robert Whattcott"

Nothing is said about the witnessing of the signing hereof. The Will might therefore have been, and I myself am perfectly certain that it was, marked with the name of William Shakspeare by the Solicitor, Fra (ncis) Collyns, who wrote the body of the Will.

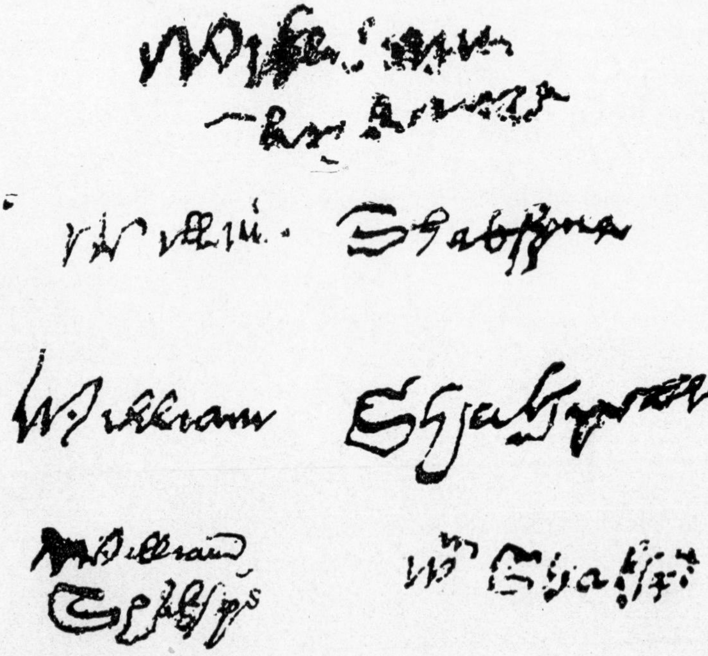

Plate XIV.

THE FIVE SO-CALLED "SHAKESPEARE SIGNATURES."

He also wrote the names of the other witnesses, which are all in the same hand-writing as the Will; shewing that Shakspeare's witnesses were also unable to write their names.

This fact, that Shakspeare's name is written by the solicitor, is conclusively proved by the recent article of Magdalene Thumm-Kintzel in the Leipzig magazine, *Der Menschenkenner*, which was published in January 1909.

In this publication, photo reproductions of certain letters in the body of the Will, and in the so-called Shakspeare signatures are placed side by side, and the evidence is irresistible that they are written by the same hand. Moreover when we remember that the Will commences "I Willim Sha *c* kspeare" with a "c" between the "a" and "k," the idea that Shakspeare himself wrote his own Will cannot be deemed worthy of serious consideration. The whole Will is in fact in the handwriting of Francis Collyns, the Warwick solicitor, who added the attestation clause.

I myself was sure that the solicitor had added the so-called signatures, when, many years ago, I examined under the strongest magnifying glasses the Will at Somerset House.

Look first at the upper writings and never again call them "signatures." The top one is on the first page of the Will, the second on the second page, the third on the last page of the Will.

The original of the top one has been very much damaged but the "W" remains quite clear. Look first only at the "W's". If the writings were signatures what could induce a man when signing his last Will to make each "W" as different from the others as possible, and why is the second Christian name written Willm?

Compare also the second and third "Shakspeare" and note that every letter is formed in a different manner. Compare the two "S's", next compare the two "h's", the "h" of the second begins at the bottom, the "h" of the third begins at the top, the same applies to the next letter the "a", so also with respect to the "k's"; how widely different these are.

Plate 14 shews at the bottom two other names also. These are taken, the one on the left from a deed of purchase of a dwelling house in Blackfriars dated March 10th 1612–13 (now in the City Library of the Corporation of London); the other on the right is from a mortgage of the same property executed on the following day, viz: March 11th 1612–13, which is now in the British Museum.

Neither of these documents states that it was "signed" but only says that it was "sealed," and it was at that date in no way necessary that any signatures should be written over the seals, but the clerks might and evidently did, place upon these deeds an abbreviated name of William Shakspeare over the seal on each document. In the case of the other two parties to the documents, the signatures are most beautifully written and are almost absolutely identical in the two deeds.

Look at these two supposititious signatures. To myself it is difficult to imagine that anyone with eyes to see could suppose them to be signatures by the same hand.

Some years ago by the courtesy of the Corporation of London, the Librarian and the Chairman of the Library Committee carried the Purchase Deed to the British Museum to place it side by side with the Mortgage Deed there.

After they had with myself and the Museum Authorities most carefully examined the two deeds, the Librarian of the City Corporation said to me, there is no reason to suppose that the Corporation deed has upon it the signature of Wm. Shakespeare, and the British Museum Authorities likewise told me that they did not think that the Museum Mortgage Deed had upon it a signature of William Shakespeare.

The more you examine the whole five the more you will be certain, as the writer is, after the most careful study of the Will and of the Deeds, that not one of the five writings is a "signature," or pretends to be a "signature," and that therefore there is a probability, practically amounting to a certainty, that the Stratford Actor could not so much as manage to scrawl his own name.

No! We possess not a scrap of writing, not even an attempt at a signature,* that can be reasonably supposed to be written by the Stratford *gentleman.*

He is styled "gentle Shakespeare": this does not refer to anything relating to his character or to his manners but it means that possessing a coat of arms he was legally entitled to call himself a "gentleman."

---

* See also Chapter XIV., p. 161.

CHAPTER IV.

Contemporary Allusions to Shackspere.

Shakspeare the Actor purchased New Place at Stratford-on-Avon in 1597 for £60 and he became a "gentleman" and an esquire when he secured a grant of arms in 1599.

How did the stage "honour" the player who had bought a coat of arms and was able to call himself a "gentleman"?

Three contemporary plays give us scenes illustrating the incident:

1st. Ben Jonson's "Every man out of his humour" which was acted in 1599 the very year of Shakspeare's grant of arms.

2nd. Shakespeare's "As you like it" which was entered at Stationers' Hall in 1600, although no copy is known to exist before the folio of 1623.

3rd. "The Return from Pernassus" which was acted at St. John's College, Cambridge in 1601, though not printed till 1606.

In addition to these three plays, there is a fourth evidence of the way in which the Clown who had purchased a coat of arms was regarded, in a pamphlet or tract of which only one copy is known to exist. This tract which can be seen in the Rylands Library, Manchester, used to be in Lord Spencer's library at Althorp, and is reprinted by Halliwell-Phillipps in "Outlines of the Life of Shakespeare," 1889, Vol. 1, pages 325-6.

Plate XV.

BACON'S CREST FROM THE BINDING OF A PRESENTATION COPY OF THE NOVUM ORGANUM, 1620.

To commence with Ben Jonson's "Every man out of his humour." The clown who had purchased a coat of arms is said to be the brother of Sordido (a miser), and is described as an "essential" clown (that is an uneducated rustic), and is styled Sogliardo which is the Italian for the filthiest possible name.

The other two characters in the scene (act iii. sc. 1) are Puntarvolo who, as his crest is a *Boar*, must be intended to represent Bacon;* and Carlo Buffone who is a buffoon or jester.

Enter Sogliardo (the filth), who is evidently the Stratford Clown, who has just purchased a coat of arms:—

Actus Tertius, Scena Prima,
Sogliardo, Punt., Carlo.

Sog. Nay I will haue him, I am resolute for that, by this Parchment Gentlemen, I haue ben so toil'd among the Harrots [meaning *Heralds*] yonder, you will not beleeue; they doe speake i' the straungest language, and giue a man the hardest termes for his money, that euer you knew.

Car. But ha' you armes? ha' your armes?

Sog. Yfaith, I thanke God I can write myselfe Gentleman now, here's my Pattent, it cost me thirtie pound by this breath.

Punt. A very faire Coat, well charg'd and full of Armorie.

Sog. Nay, it has as much varietie of colours in it, as you haue seene a Coat haue, how like you the Crest, Sir?

Punt. I vnderstand it not well, what is 't?

---

* Through the whole play the fact that Puntarvolo represents Bacon is continually apparent to the instructed reader. Note especially Act II., Scene 3, where Puntarvolo addresses his wife, who appears at a window, in a parody of the address of Romeo to Juliet. Again in Act II., Scene 3, Carlo Buffone calls Puntarvolo "A yeoman pheuterer." Pheuter or feuter means a rest or support for a spear—which is informing.

Sog. Marry Sir, it is your Bore without a head Rampant.

Punt. A Bore without a head, that 's very rare.

Car. I, [Aye] and Rampant too: troth I commend the Herald's wit, he has deciphered him well: A Swine without a head, without braine, wit, anything indeed, Ramping to Gentilitie. You can blazon the rest signior? can you not?

. . . . . .

. . . . . .

Punt. Let the word be, *Not without mustard*, your Crest is very rare sir.

Shakspeare's "word" that is his "motto" was—non sanz droict— not without right — and I desire the reader also especially to remember Sogliardo's words "Yfaith I thanke God" a phrase which though it appears in the quartos is changed in the 1616 Ben Jonson folio into "I thank *them*" which has no meaning.

Next we turn to Shakespeare's "As you like it." This play, though entered at Stationers' Hall in 1600 and probably played quite as early, is not known in print till it appeared in the folio of 1623. The portion to which I wish to refer is the commencement of Actus Quintus, Scena Prima.

Act 5, Scene 1.

Enter Clowne and Awdrie.

Clow. We shall finde a time *Awdrie*, patience gentle Awdrie.

Awd. Faith the priest was good enough, for all the olde gentlemans saying.

Clow. A most wicked Sir *Oliver*, *Awdrie*, a most vile *Mar-text*. But *Awdrie*, there is a youth heere in the forrest layes claime to you.

Awd. I, I know who 'tis: he hath no interest in mee in the world: here comes the man you meane.

(Enter William)

Clo. It is meat and drinke to me to see a clowne, by my troth, we that haue good wits, haue much to answer for: we shall be flouting: we cannot hold.

Will. Good eu'n *Audrey*.

Awd. God ye good eu'n *William*.

Will. And good eu'n to you sir.

Clo. Good eu'n gentle friend. Couer thy head, couer thy head: Nay prethee bee couer'd. How olde are you Friend?

Will. Fiue and twentie Sir.

Clo. A ripe age: Is thy name *William?*

Will. *William*, Sir.

Clo. A faire name. Was't borne i' the Forrest heere?

Will. I [Aye] Sir, I thanke God.

Clo. Thanke God: A good answer: Art rich?

Will. 'Faith Sir, so, so.

Clo. So, so, is good, very good, very excellent good: and yet it is not, it is but so, so: Art thou wise?

Will. I [Aye] sir, I haue a prettie wit.

Clo. Why, thou saist well. I do now remember a saying: The Foole doth thinke he is wise, but the wise man knowes himselfe to be a Foole. . . . . . . You do loue this maid?

Will. I do Sir.

Clo. Giue me your hand: art thou Learned?

Will. No Sir.

Clo. Then learne this of me, To haue is to haue. For it is a figure in Rhetoricke, that drink being powr'd out of a cup into a glasse, by filling the one, doth empty the other. For all your Writers do consent, that *ipse* is hee: now you are not *ipse*, for I am he.

Will. Which he Sir?

Clo. He Sir, that must marrie this woman.

Firstly I want to call your attention to Touchstone the courtier who is playing clown and who we are told "uses his folly like a stalking horse and under the presentation of that he shoots his wit." Notice that Touchstone refuses to be married to Awdrey (who probably represents the plays of Shakespeare) by a *Mar-text*, and she declares that the Clown William "has no interest in mee in the world." William—shall we say Shakspeare of Stratford?—enters and is greeted as "gentle" (*i.e.* he is possessed of a coat of arms). He says "Thank God" he was born in the forest here (Ardennes, very near in sound to Arden)*. "Thank God" is repeated by Touchstone and as it is the same phrase that is used by Sogliardo in Ben Jonson's play I expect that it was an ejaculation very characteristic of the real man of Stratford and I

* There was a forest of Arden in Warwickshire.

am confirmed in this belief because in the folio edition of Ben Jonson's plays the phrase is changed to "I thank *them*" which has no meaning.

The clown of Ardennes is rich but only rich for a clown (Shakspeare of Stratford was not really rich, New Place cost only £60).

Asked if he is wise, he says "aye," that is "yes," and adds that he has "a pretty wit," a phrase we must remember that is constantly used in reference to the Stratford actor. Touchstone mocks him with a paraphrase of the well-known maxim "If you are wise you are a Foole if you be a Foole you are wise" which is to be found in Bacon's "Advancement of Learning" Antitheta xxxi. Then he asks him "*Art thou learned*" and William replies "*No sir.*" This means, *unquestionably*, as every lawyer must know, that William replies that he cannot *read* one line of print. I feel sure the man called Sha*c*kspeare of Stratford was an uneducated rustic, never able to read a single line of print, and that this is the reason why no books were found in his house, this is the reason why his solicitor, Thomas Greene, lived with him in his house at New Place (Halliwell-Phillipps: Outlines, 1889, Vol. 1, p. 226);—a well-known fact that very much puzzles those who do not realize the depth of Shakspeare's illiteracy.

CHAPTER V.

"The Return from Pernassus" and "Ratsei's Ghost."

THE next play to which attention must be called is "The Return from Pernassus" which was produced at Cambridge in 1601 and was printed in 1606 with the following title page:—

The Returne from Pernassus
or
The Scourge of Simony.
Publiquely acted by the Students
in Saint Johns Colledge in
Cambridge.
At London
Printed by G. Eld for John Wright, and
are to bee sold at his shop at
Christchurch Gate.
1606.

The portion to which I wish to direct attention is:—

Actus 5, Scena 1.

Studioso. Fayre fell good *Orpheus*, that would rather be

King of a mole hill, then a Keysars slaue:
Better it is mongst fidlers to be chiefe,
Then at plaiers trencher beg reliefe.
But ist not strange this mimick apes should prize
Vnhappy Schollers at a hireling rate.
Vile world, that lifts them vp to hye degree,
And treades vs downe in groueling misery.
England affordes those glorious vagabonds,
That carried earst their fardels on their backes,
Coursers to ride on through the gazing streetes
Sooping it in their glaring Satten sutes,
And Pages to attend their maisterships:
With mouthing words that better wits haue framed,
They purchase lands, and now Esquiers are made.

Philomusus. What ere they seeme being euen at the best
They are but sporting fortunes *scornfull* iests.

Can these last two lines refer to Shakspeare the actor seeming to be the poet? Note that they are spoken by Philomusus that is friend of the poetic muse. Mark also the words "this mimick apes." Notice especially "with mouthing words that *better* wits haue framed, they purchase lands and now Esquiers are made" *i.e.* get grants of arms. Who at this period among mimics excepting W. Shakspeare of Stratford purchased lands and obtained also a grant of arms?

That this sneer "mouthing words that better wits have framed" must have been aimed at Shakspeare is strongly confirmed by the tract (reprinted by Halliwell-Phillipps in his "Outlines of Shakespeare," 1889, Vol. 1, p. 325) which is called "Ratsei's Ghost or the second part of his mad prankes and Robberies."

This pamphlet bears no date, but was entered at Stationers' Hall May 31st 1605. There is only a single copy in existence, which used to be in Earl Spencer's library at Althorp but is now in the Rylands Library at Manchester. As I said, it is reprinted by Halliwell-Phillipps, and Stratfordians are obliged to agree with him that the reference is unquestionably to "Wm Shakespeare of Stratford." The most important part which is spoken by Ratsei the robber to a country player is as follows:—

Ratsei. And for you sirra, saies hee to the chiefest of them, thou hast a good presence upon a stage; methinks thou darkenst thy merite by playing in the country. Get thee to London, for if one man were dead, they will have much neede of such a one as thou art. There would be none in my opinion fitter then thyselfe to play his parts. My conceipt is such of thee, that I durst venture all the mony in my purse on thy head to play Hamlet with him for a wager. There thou

> shalt learn to be frugall,—for players were never so thriftie as they are now about London—and to feed upon all men, to let none feede upon thee; to make thy hand a stranger to thy pocket, thy hart slow to performe thy tongues promise, and when thou feelest thy purse well lined, buy thee some place of lordship in the country, that, growing weary of playing, thy mony may there bring thee to dignitie and reputation; then thou needest care for no man, nor not for them that before made thee prowd with speaking their words upon the stage.

The whole account of buying a place in the country, of feeding upon all men (that is lending money upon usury) of never keeping promises, of never giving anything in charity, agrees but too well with the few records we possess of the man of Stratford. And therefore Stratfordians are obliged to accept Halliwell-Phillipps' dictum that this tract called Ratsei's Ghost refers to the actor of Stratford and that "*he* needed not to care for them that before made *him* proud with speaking *their* words upon the stage." How is it possible that Stratfordians can continue to refuse to admit that the statement in the "Return from Pernassus" "with mouthing words that better wits haue framed they purchase lands and now Esquiers are made" must also refer to the Stratford Actor?

CHAPTER VI.

Shackspere's Correspondence!

THERE is only a single letter extant addressed to Shakspeare, and this asks for a loan of £30! It is dated 25th October 1598, and is from Richard Quiney.* It reads

"Loveinge Countreyman I am bolde of yo^{w} as of a ffrende, "craveinge yo^{wr} helpe w^{t}h xxx^{ll} vppon m^{r} Bushells & my "securytee or m^{r} Myttons w^{t}h me. m^{r} Rosswell is nott come "to London as yeate & I have especiall cawse. yo^{w} shall "ffrende me muche in helpeinge me out of all the debettes I "owe in London I thancke god & muche quiet my mynde w^{c}h "wolde nott be indebeted I am nowe towardes the Cowrte in "hope of answer for the dispatche of my Buysenes. yo^{w} shall "nether loase creddytt nor monney by me the Lorde wyllinge "and nowe butt perswade yo^{wr} selfe soe as I hope & yo^{w} shall "nott need to feare butt w^{t}h all hartie thanckefullenes I wyll "holde my tyme & content yo^{wr} ffrende & yf we Bargaine "farther yo^{w} shalbe the paie m^{r} yo^{wr} selfe. my tyme biddes me "hasten to an ende & soe I committ thys [to] yo^{wr} care & hope "of yo^{wr} helpe. I feare I shall nott be backe thys night ffrom "the Cowrte. haste. the Lorde be w^{t}h yo^{w} & with us all amen "ffrom the Bell in Carter Lane the 25 October 1598.

"yo^{wrs} in all kyndenes
"Ryc. Quyney

(*addressed*)

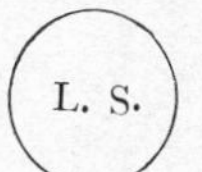

"To my Loveinge good ffrend
"& contreymann m^{r} w^{m}
"Shackespere d [e] l [ive] r thees."

---

* This Richard Quyney's son Thomas married 10th February 1616, Judith, William Shakespeare's younger daughter, who, like her father, the supposed poet, was totally illiterate, and signed the Register with a mark.

This letter is the only letter known to exist which was ever addressed to William Shackspere, the illiterate householder of Stratford, who as has been pointed out in these pages was totally unable to read a line of print, or to write even his own name. There are however in existence three, and three only, contemporary letters referring in any way to him, and these are not about literature with which the Stratford man had nothing whatever to do—but about mean and sordid small business transactions.

One is from Master Abraham Sturley, who writes in 1598 to a friend in London in reference to Shakspeare lending "Some monei on some od yarde land or other att Shottri or neare about us."

Another is dated Nov. 4th 1598, and is from the same Abraham Sturley to Richard Quiney in which we are told that "our countriman Mr Wm Shak would procure us monei wc I will like of."

A third from Adrian Quiney written (about 1598-1599) to his son Rycharde Quiney in which he says "yff yow bargen with Wm Sha or receve money therfor, brynge youre money homme."

There exists no contemporary letter from anyone to anyone, referring to the Stratford actor as being a poet or as being in any way connected with literature. But from the Court Records we learn that;

In 1600 Shakespeare brought action against John Clayton in London for £7 and got judgment in his favour. He also sued Philip Rogers of Stratford for two shillings loaned.

In 1604 he sued Philip Rogers for several bushels of malt sold to him at various times between March 27th and the end of May of that year, amounting in all to the value of £1. 15s. 10d. The poet a dealer in malt?

In 1608 he prosecuted John Addenbroke to recover a debt of £6 and sued his surety Horneby.

Halliwell-Phillipps tells us that "The precepts as appears from memoranda in the originals, were issued by the poet's solicitor Thomas Greene who was then residing under some unknown conditions* at New Place"

Referring to these sordid stories, Richard Grant White, that strong believer in the Stratford man, says in his "Life and genius of William Shakespeare," p. 156 "The pursuit of an impoverished man for the sake of imprisoning him and depriving him both of the power of paying his debts and supporting himself and his family, is an incident in Shakespeare's life which it requires the utmost allowance and consideration for the practice of the time and country to enable us to contemplate with equanimity—satisfaction is impossible."

"The biographer of Shakespeare must record these facts because the literary antiquaries have unearthed and brought them forward as new particulars of the life of Shakespeare. We hunger and receive these husks; we open our mouths for food and we break our teeth against these stones."

* This fact so puzzling to Halliwell-Phillipps is fully explained when it is realised that William Shackspere of Stratford could neither read or write.

Yes! The world has broken its teeth too long upon these stones to continue to mistake them for bread. And as the accomplished scholar and poetess the late Miss Anna Swanwick once declared to the writer, she knew nothing of the Bacon and Shakespeare controversy, but Mr. Sidney Lee's "Life of Shakespeare" had convinced her that his man never wrote the plays. And that is just what everybody else is saying at Eton, at Oxford, at Cambridge, in the Navy, in the Army, and pretty generally among unprejudiced people everywhere, who are satisfied, as is Mark Twain, that the most learned of works could not have been written by the most *un*learned of men.

Yes! It does matter that the "Greatest Birth of Time" should no longer be considered to have been the work of the unlettered rustic of Stratford; and the hour has at last come when it should be universally known that this mighty work was written by the man who had taken all knowledge for his province, the man who said "I have, though in a despised weed [that is under a Pseudonym] procured the good of all men"; the man who left his "name and memory to men's charitable speeches, and to foreign nations, and the next ages."

CHAPTER VII.

Bacon acknowledged to be a Poet.

In discussing the question of the Authorship of the plays many people appear to be unaware that Bacon was considered by his contemporaries to be a great poet. It seems therefore advisable to quote a few witnesses who speak of his pre-eminence in poetry.

In 1645 there was published "The Great Assises holden in Parnassus by Apollo and his assessours" a facsimile of the title of which is given on page 57. This work is anonymous but is usually ascribed to George Withers and in it Bacon as Lord Verulan is placed first and designated "Chancellor of Parnassus" that is "Greatest of Poets."

After the title, the book commences with two pages of which facsimiles are given on pages 58, 59.

Apollo appears at the top, next comes Lord Verulan as Chancellor of Parnassus, Sir Philip Sidney and other world renowned names follow and then below the line side by side is a list of the jurors and a list of the malefactors.

A little examination will teach us that the jurors are really the same persons as the malefactors and that we ought to read right across the page as if the dividing line did not exist.

Acting on this principle we perceive that George Wither [Withers] is correctly described as Mercurius Britanicus. Mr. Sidney Lee tells us that Withers regarded "Britain's Remembrancer" 1628 and "Prosopopaeia Britannica" 1648 as his greatest works.

Thomas Cary [Carew] is correctly described as Mercurias Aulicus—Court Messenger. He went to the French Court with Lord Herbert and was made Gentleman of the Privy Chamber by Charles I who presented him with an estate at Sunninghill.

Thomas May is correctly described as Mercurius Civicus. He applied for the post of Chronologer to the City of London and James I wrote to the Lord Mayor (unsuccessfully) in his favour.

Josuah Sylvester is correctly described as The Writer of Diurnals. He translated Du Bartas "Divine Weekes," describing day by day, that is "Diurnally," the creation of the world.

Georges Sandes [Sandys] is The Intelligencer. He travelled all over the world and his book of travels was one of the popular works of the period.

Michael Drayton is The Writer of Occurrences. Besides the "Poly-Olbion" he wrote "England's Heroicall Epistles" and "The Barron's Wars."

Francis Beaumont is The Writer of Passages. This exactly describes him as he is known as writing in conjunction with Fletcher. "Beamount and Fletcher make one poet, they single dare not adventure on a play."

12.

THE GREAT ASSISES Holden in *PARNASSVS* BY APOLLO AND HIS ASSESSOVRS:

At which Seſſions are Arraigned

Mercurius Britanicus.
Mercurius Aulicus.
Mercurius Civicus.
The Scout.
The writer of Diurnalls.
The Intelligencer.
The writer of Occurrences.
The writer of Paſſages.
The Poſt.
The Spye.
The writer of weekly Accounts.
The Scottiſh Dove, &c.

LONDON,
Printed by *Richard Cotes*, for *Edward Husbands*, and are to be ſold at his Shop in the *Middle Temple*, 1645.

Plate XVI.

Facsimile Title Page.

The Lord VERVLAN, *Chancellor of Parnaſſus.*

Sir PHILIP SIDNEY, *High Conſtable of Par.*

WILLIAM BVDEVS, *High Treaſurer.*

JOHN PICVS, *Earle of* Mirandula, *High Chamberlaine.*

JVLIVS CESAR SCALIGER

ERASMUS ROTERODAM.

JUSTUS LIPSIUS

JOHN BARCKLAY

JOHN BODINE

ADRIAN TVRNEBVS

ISAAC CASAVBON

JOHN SELDEN

HVGO GROTIVS

DANIEL HEINSIVS

CONRADVS VOSSIVS

AUGUSTINE MASCARDUS

The Jurours.

George Wither
Thomas Cary
Thomas May
William Davenant
Joſuah Sylveſter
Georges Sandes
Michael Drayton
Francis Beaumont
John Fletcher
Thomas Haywood
William Shakeſpeere
Philip Maſsinger.

The Malefactours.

Mercurius Britanicus
Mercurias Aulicus
Mercurius Civicus
The Scout
The writer of Diurnals
The Intelligencer
The writer of Occurrences
The writer of Paſſages
The Poſte
The Spye
The writer of weekely Accounts
The Scottiſh Dove,&c.

A 2 Jo-

Plate XVII.

FACSIMILE OF PAGE III OF "THE GREAT ASSISES."

JOSEPH SCALIGER, the Censour of manners in *Parnassus*.	
	EDMVND SPENCER, Clerk of the Assises.
BEN. JOHNSON, Keeper of the Trophonian Denne.	
JOHN TAYLOVR, Cryer of the Court.	

THE

Plate XVIII.

FACSIMILE OF PAGE IV OF "THE GREAT ASSISES."

Plate XVIII.

FACSIMILE OF PAGE IV. OF "THE GREAT ASSISES."

William Shakespeere is "The writer of weekely accounts." This exactly describes him, for the only literature for which he was responsible was the accounts sent out by his clerk or attorney.

Turning over the pages of the little book on page 9 the cryer calls out "Then Sylvester, Sands, Drayton, Beaumont, Fletcher, Massinger, Shakespeare (sic) and Heywood, Poets good and true." This statement seems to be contradicted so far as Shakespeare is concerned by the defendant who says on page 31 "Shakespear's (sic) a mimicke" (that is a mere actor not a poet).

"Beamount and Fletcher make one poet, they
Single, dare not adventure on a play."

Each of these statements seems to be true. And on page 33 Apollo* says

"We should to thy exception give consent
But since we are assur'd, 'tis thy intent,
By this refusall, onely to deferre
That censure, which our justice must conferre
Upon thy merits; we must needs decline
From approbation of these pleas of thine."

That is, Apollo *admits* that Shakespeare is not a poet but a "mimic," the word to which I called your attention in the "Return from Pernassus" in relation to "this mimick apes." In this little book Shakespeare's name occurs three times, and on each occasion is spelled differently.

---

* The words attributed to Apollo, are of course spoken by his Chancellor Bacon. See note on the number 33 on page 112.

This clear statement that the actor Shakespeare was not a poet but only a tradesman who sent out his "weekly accounts" is, I think, here for the first time pointed out. It seems very difficult to conceive of a much higher testimony to Bacon's pre-eminence in poetry than the fact that he is placed as "Chancellor of Parnassus" under Apollo. But a still higher position is accorded to him when it is suggested that Apollo feared that he himself should lose his crown which would be placed on Bacon's head.

Walter Begbie in "Is it Shakespeare?" 1903, p. 274, tells us:—That Thomas Randolf, in Latin verses published in 1640 but probably written some 14 years earlier says that Phœbus was accessory to Bacon's death because he was afraid lest Bacon should some day come to be crowned King of poetry or the Muses. Farther on the same writer declares that as Bacon "was himself a singer" he did not need to be celebrated in song by others, and that George Herbert calls Bacon the colleague of Sol [Phœbus Apollo].

George Herbert was himself a dramatic poet and Bacon dedicated his "Translation of the Psalms" to him "who has overlooked so many of my works."

Mr. Begbie also tells us that Thomas Campion addresses Bacon thus "Whether the thorny volume of the Law or the Schools or the *Sweet Muse* allure thee."

It may be worth while here to quote the similar testimony which is borne by John Davies of Hereford who in his "Scourge of Folly" published about 1610, writes

"To the royall, ingenious, and all-learned
Knight,—

Sr Francis Bacon.

Thy *bounty* and the *Beauty* of thy Witt
Comprisd in Lists of *Law* and learned *Arts*,
Each making thee for great *Imployment* fitt
Which now thou hast, (though short of thy
deserts)
Compells my pen to let fall shining *Inke*
And to bedew the *Baies* that *deck* thy *Front*;
And to thy health in *Helicon* to drinke
As to her *Bellamour* the *Muse* is wont:
For thou dost her embozom; and dost vse
Her company for sport twixt grave affaires;
So vtterst Law the liuelyer through thy *Muse*.
And for that all thy *Notes* are sweetest *Aires*;
My Muse thus notes thy worth in eu'ry Line,
With yncke which thus she sugers; so, to shine."

But nothing can much exceed in value the testimony of Ben Jonson who in his "Discoveries," 1641, says "But his learned, and able (though unfortunate) *Successor* [Bacon in margin] is he, who hath fill'd up all numbers, and perform'd that in our tongue, which may be compar'd or preferr'd either to insolent *Greece*, or haughty *Rome*."

"He who hath filled up all numbers"* means unquestionably "He that hath written every kind of poetry."

Alexander Pope the poet declares that he himself "lisped in numbers for the numbers came." Ben Jonson therefore bears testimony to the fact that Bacon was so great a poet that he had in poetry written that "which may be compar'd or preferr'd either to insolent *Greece* or haughty *Rome*."

But in 1623 Ben Jonson had said of the AUTHOR of the plays

> "*Or when thy sockes were on*
> *Leaue thee alone, for the comparison*
> *Of all, that insolent* Greece *or haughtie* Rome
> *Sent forth, or since did from their ashes come.*"

Surely the statements in the "Discoveries" were

---

*While I am perfectly satisfied that the above explanation of the meaning of the expression "All numbers" is the correct one; I am not unaware that at the date at which the Discoveries appeared "All numbers" would be generally understood in its classical sense; Jonson of course not being permitted to speak too plainly. He was foreman of Bacon's good pens and one of his "left-hands"; as any visitor to Westminster Abbey may learn, the attendants there being careful to point out that the sculptor has "accidentally" clothed Jonson's Bust in a left-handed coat. (With respect to the meaning of this the reader is referred to Plate 33, page 131.) Thus far was written and in print when the writer's attention was called to the Rev. George O Neill's little brochure, "Could Bacon have written the plays?" in which in a note to page 14 we find "Numeri" in Latin, "numbers" in English, applied to literature mean nothing else than verse, and even seem to exclude prose. Thus Tibullus writes, "*Numeris ille hic pede libero scribit* (one writes in verse another in prose), and Shakespeare has the same antithesis in "Love's Labour Lost" (iv., 3), "These numbers I will tear and write in prose." Yet all this does not settle the matter, for "Numeri" is also used in the sense merely of "parts" Pliny speaks of a prose work as perfect in all its parts, "*Omnibus numeris absolutus*," and Cicero says of a plan of life, "*Omnes numeros virtutis continet*" (it contains every element of virtue). So that Jonson may have merely meant to say in slightly pedantic phrase that Bacon had passed away all parts fulfilled.

intended to tell us who was the AUTHOR of the plays.

After perusing these contemporary evidences, and they might be multiplied,* it is difficult to understand how anyone can venture to dispute Bacon's position as preeminent in poetry. But it may be of interest to those who doubt whether Bacon (irrespective of any claim to the authorship of the plays) could be deemed to be a great poet, to quote here the words of Percy Bysshe Shelley, who in his "Defence of Poetry" says

"Bacon was a poet. His language has a sweet and majestic rhythm, which satisfies the sense, no less than the almost superhuman wisdom of his philosophy satisfies the intellect. It is a strain which distends and then bursts the circumference of the reader's mind, and pours itself forth together with it into the universal element with which it has perpetual sympathy."

The immortal plays are the "Greatest Birth of Time," and contain a short summary of the wisdom of the world from ancient times, and they exhibit an extent and depth of knowledge in every branch which has never been equalled at any period of the world's history. In classic lore, as the late Mr. Churton Collins recently pointed out, they evince the ripest scholarship. And this is confirmed by classical scholars all the world over.

None but the profoundest lawyers can realise the extent of the knowledge not only of the theory but of

* In 1615, although nothing of poetical importance bearing Bacon's name had been published, we find in Stowe's "Annales," p. 811, that Bacon's name appears seventh in the list there given of Elizabethan poets.

the practice of Law which is displayed. Lord Campbell says that Lord Eldon [supposed to have been the most learned of judges] need not have been ashamed of the law of Shakespeare. And as an instance of the way in which the members of the legal profession look up to the mighty author I may mention that some years ago, at a banquet of a Shakespeare Society at which Mr. Sidney Lee and the writer were present, the late Mr. Crump, Q.C., editor of the *Law Times*, who probably possessed as much knowledge of law as any man in this country, declared that to tell him that the plays were not written by the greatest lawyer the world has ever seen, or ever would see, was to tell him what he had sufficient knowledge of law to know to be nonsense. He said also that he was not ashamed to confess that he himself, though he had some reputation for knowledge of law, did not possess sufficient legal knowledge to realise one quarter of the law that was contained in the Shakespeare plays.

It requires a philologist to fully appreciate what the enormous vocabulary employed in the plays implies.

Max Müller in his "Science of Language," Vol. 1, 1899, p. 379, says

"A well-educated person in England, who has been at a public school and at the University . . . seldom uses more than about 3,000 or 4,000 words. . . . The Hebrew Testament says all that it has to say with 5,642 words, Milton's poetry is built up with 8,000; and Shakespeare, who probably displayed a greater variety of expression than any writer in any language . . . produced all his plays with about 15,000 words."

Shakspeare the householder of Stratford could not have known so many as one thousand words.

But Bacon declared that we must make our English language capable of conveying the highest thoughts, and by the plays he has very largely created what we now call the English language. The plays and the sonnets also reveal their author's life.

In the play of "Hamlet" especially, Bacon seems to tell us a good deal concerning himself, for the autobiographical character of that play is clearly apparent to those who have eyes to see. I will, however, refer only to a single instance in that play. In the Quarto of 1603, which is the first known edition of the play of "Hamlet," we are told, in the scene at the grave, that Yorick has been dead a dozen years; but in the 1604 Quarto, which was printed in the following year, Yorick is stated to have been dead twenty-three years. This corrected number, twenty-three, looks therefore like a real date of the death of a real person. The words in the Quarto of 1604 are as follows:—

Hamlet, Act v, Scene i.

"[Grave digger called.] Clow [n] . . . heer's a scull "now hath lyen you i' th' earth 23 yeeres . . . this "same scull, sir, was, sir, *Yorick's* skull, the Kings "jester . . .

"*Ham* [*let*]. Alas poore *Yoricke*, I knew him "*Horatio*, a fellow of infinite iest, of most excellent "fancie, hee hath bore me on his backe a thousand "times . . . Heere hung those lyppes that I haue "kist, I know not howe oft, where be your gibes now? "your gamboles, your songs, your flashes of merriment, "that were wont to set the table on a roare, not one "now to mocke your owne grinning . . ."

The King's Jester who died about 1580-1, just twenty-three years before 1604 (as stated in the play), was John Heywood, the last of the King's Jesters. The words spoken by Hamlet exactly describe John Heywood, who was wont to set the table in a roar with his jibes, his gambols, his songs, and his flashes of merriment. He was a favourite at the English Court during three if not four reigns, and it is recorded that Queen Elizabeth as a Princess rewarded him. It is an absolutely gratuitous assumption that he was obliged permanently to leave England when she became Queen. Indeed it is believed that he was an intimate friend of the Bacon family, and must have carried little Francis Bacon any number of times upon his back, and the little fellow must have kissed him still more oftentimes. The story in the play of "Hamlet" seems, therefore, to fit in exactly with the facts of Bacon's life; but it is not possible that the most fertile imagination of the most confirmed Stratfordian can suppose that the Stratford actor ever saw John Heywood, who died long before Shakspere came to London.

CHAPTER VIII.

The Author revealed in the Sonnets.

Bacon also reveals much of himself in the play "As you like it," which of course means "Wisdom from the mouth of a fool." In that play, besides giving us much valuable information concerning his "mask" William Shakespeare, he also tells us why it was necessary for him to write under a pseudonym.

Speaking in the character of Jaques, who is the alter ego of Touchstone, he says,

Act ii, Scene 7.

"O that I were a foole,
I am ambitious for a motley coat.
Duke. Thou shalt haue one.
Jaq. It is my onely suite,
Prouided that you weed your better iudgements
Of all opinion that growes ranke in them,
That I am wise. I must haue liberty
Wiithall, as large a Charter as the winde,
To blow on whom I please, for so fooles haue:
And they that are most gauled with my folly,
They most must laugh. . . . . .
Inuest me in my motley: Giue me leaue

To speake my minde, and I will through and through
Cleanse the foule bodie of th' infected world
If they will patiently receiue my medicine."

He also gives us most valuable information in Sonnet 81.

Or I shall liue your Epitaph to make,
Or you suruiue when I in earth am rotten,
From hence your memory death cannot take,
Although in me each part will be forgotten,
Your name from hence immortall life shall haue,
Though I (once gone) to all the world must dye,
The Earth can yeeld me but a common graue,
When you intombed in men's eyes shall lye,
Your monument shall be my gentle verse,
Which eyes not yet created shall ore read,
And toungs to be, your being shall rehearse,
When all the breathers of this world are dead,
You still shall liue (such vertue hath my Pen)
Where breath most breaths euen in the mouths of men.

Stratfordians tell us that the above is written in reference to a poet whom Shakespeare "evidently" regarded as a rival. But it is difficult to imagine how sensible men can satisfy their reason with such an explanation. Is it possible to conceive that a poet should write *against* a *rival*

"Your name from hence immortall life shall haue
Though I (once gone) to all the world must dye"

or should say *against* a *rival,*

> "The Earth can yeeld me but a common graue
> While you intombed in men's eyes shall lye."

or should have declared "*against* a *rival,*"

> "Your monument shall be my gentle verse"

No! This sonnet is evidently written in reference to the writer's mask or pseudonym which would continue to have immortal life (even though he himself might be forgotten) as he says

> "Although in me each part will be forgotten."

It is sometimes said that Shakespeare (meaning the Stratford actor) did not know the value of his immortal works. Is that true of the writer of this sonnet who says

> "my gentle verse
> Which eyes not yet created shall ore read"

No! The writer knew his verses were immortal and would immortalize the pseudonym attached to them

> "When all the breathers of this world are dead."

Perhaps the reader will better understand Sonnet 81 if I insert the words necessary to fully explain it.

> Or shall I [Bacon] live your Epitaph to make,
> Or you [Shakespeare] survive when I in Earth am rotten,
> From hence your memory death cannot take,
> Although in me each part will be forgotten.
> Your name [Shakespeare] from hence immortal life shall have,

Though I [Bacon] once gone to all the world
must die,
The earth can yield me but a common grave,
When you entombed in men's eyes shall lie,
Your monument shall be my [not your] gentle
verse,
Which eyes not yet created shall ore read,
And tongues to be your being [which as an author
was not] shall rehearse,
When all the breathers of this world are dead,
You [Shakespeare] still shall live, such vertue
hath my pen [not your own pen, for you never
wrote a line]
Where breathe most breaths even in the mouths
of men.

This Sonnet was probably written considerably earlier than 1609, but at that date Bacon's name had not been attached to any work of great literary importance.

After the writer had learned the true meaning of Sonnet 81, his eyes were opened to the inward meaning of other Sonnets, and he perceived that Sonnet No. 76 repeated the same tale.

"Why write I still all one, euer the same,
And keep inuention in a noted weed,
That euery word doth almost sel my name,
Shewing their birth and where they did proceed?"

(Sel may mean spell or tell or possibly betray.)

Especially note that "Invention" is the same word that is used by Bacon in his letter to Sir Tobie Matthew of 1609 (same date as the Sonnets), and also especially remark the phrase "in a noted weed," which means in a "pseudonym," and compare it with the words of Bacon's prayer, "I have (though in a 'despised weed') procured the good of all men." [Resuscitatio, 1671.] Was not the pseudonym of the Actor Shakespeare a very "despised weed" in those days?

Let us look also at Sonnet No. 78.

> "So oft have I enuoked thee for my Muse,
> And found such faire assistance in my verse,
> As every *alien* pen hath got my use,
> And under thee their poesy disperse."

Here again we should understand how to read this Sonnet as under:—

> "So oft have I enuoked thee [Shakespeare] for my Muse,
> And found such faire assistance in my verse,
> As every *alien* pen hath got my use,
> And under thee [Shakespeare] their poesy disperse."

"Shakespeare" is frequently charged with being careless of his works and indifferent to the piracy of his name; but we see by this Sonnet, No. 78, that the real author was not indifferent to the false use of his pseudonym, though it was, of course, impossible for him to take any effectual action if he desired to preserve his incognito, his mask, his pseudonym.

CHAPTER IX.

Mr. Sidney Lee and the Stratford Bust.

ONE word to the Stratfordians. The "Shakespeare of Stratford-on-Avon" myth has been shattered and destroyed by the mass of inexactitudes collected in the supposititious "Life of Shakespeare" by Mr. Sidney Lee, who has done his best to pulverise what remained of that myth by recently writing as follows:—

"Most of those who have pressed the question [of Bacon being the real Shake-speare] on my notice, are men of acknowledged intelligence and reputation in their own branch of life, both at home and abroad. I therefore desire as respectfully, but also as emphatically and as publicly, as I can, to put on record the fact, as one admitting to my mind of no rational ground for dispute, that there exists every manner of contemporary evidence to prove that Shakspere, the householder of Stratford-on-Avon, wrote with his own hand, and exclusively by the light of his only genius (merely to paraphrase the contemporary inscription on his tomb in Stratford-on-Avon Church) those dramatic works which form the supreme achievement in English Literature."

As a matter of fact, not a single scrap of evidence,

contemporary or otherwise, exists to show that Shakspere, the householder of Stratford-on-Avon, wrote the plays or anything else; indeed, the writer thinks that he has conclusively proved that this child of illiterate parents and father of an illiterate child was himself so illiterate that he was never able to write so much as his own name. But Mr. Sidney Lee seems prepared to accept *anything* as "contemporary evidence," for on pages 276–7 (1898 edition) of his "Life of Shakespeare" he writes

"Before 1623 an elaborate monument, by a London sculptor of Dutch birth, Gerard Johnson, was erected to Shakespeare's memory in the chancel of the parish church. It includes a half-length bust, depicting the dramatist on the point of writing. The fingers of the right hand are disposed as if holding a pen, and under the left hand lies a quarto sheet of paper."

As a matter of fact, the *present* Stratford monument was not put up till about one hundred and twenty years *after* Shakspeare's death. The original monument, see Plate 3 on Page 8, was a very different monument, and the figure, as I have shewn in Plate 5, instead of holding a pen in its hand, rests its two hands on a wool-sack or cushion. Of course, the false bust in the existing monument was substituted for the old bust for the purpose of fraudulently supporting the Stratford myth.

When Mr. Sidney Lee wrote that the present monument was erected before 1623 he did not do this consciously to deceive the public; still, it is difficult to pardon him for this and the other reckless statements with which his book is filled. But what are we to say of his words (respecting the *present* monument) which we read on page 286? "It was first engraved—very imperfectly—in Rowe's edition of 1709." An exact full size photo facsimile reproduction of Rowe's engraving is shown in Plate 19, Page 77.

As a matter of fact, the real Stratford monument of 1623 was first engraved in Dugdale's "Warwickshire" of 1656, where it appears opposite to page 523. We can, however, pardon Mr. Sidney Lee for his ignorance of the existence of that engraving; but how shall we pardon him for citing Rowe as a witness to the early existence of the present bust? To anyone not wilfully blinded by passion and prejudice, Rowe's engraving [see Plate 19, Page 77] clearly shews a figure absolutely different from the Bust in the present monument. Rowe's figure is in the same attitude as the Bust of the original monument engraved by Dugdale, and does not hold a pen in its hand, but its two hands are supported on a wool-sack or cushion, in the same manner as in the Bust from Dugdale which I have shewn in Plate 5, on Page 14.

What are we to say respecting the frontispiece to the 1898 edition of what he is pleased to describe as the "Life of William Shakespeare," which Mr. Sidney Lee tells us is "from the 'Droeshout' painting now in the Shakespeare Memorial Gallery at Stratford-on-Avon"?

As a matter of fact there is no "Droeshout"

Plate XIX.

THE ORIGINAL STRATFORD MONUMENT, FROM ROWE'S LIFE OF SHAKESPEARE, 1709.

Plate XIX.

The Original Stratford Monument, from Rowe's Life of Shakespeare, 1709.

painting. The picture falsely so called is a manifest forgery and a palpable fraud, for in it all the revealing marks of the engraving by Martin Droeshout which appeared in the 1623 folio are purposely omitted. A full size photo facsimile of Martin Droeshout's engraving is shewn in Plate 8, pp. 20-21. In the false and fraudulent painting we find no double line to shew the mask, and the coat is really a coat and not a garment cunningly composed of two left arms.

Still it does seem singularly appropriate and peculiarly fitting that Mr. Sidney Lee should have selected as the frontispiece of the romance which he calls the "Life" of Shakespeare, an engraving of the false and fraudulent painting now in the Stratford-on-Avon Gallery for his first edition of 1898; and should also have selected an engraving of the false and fraudulent monument now in Stratford-on-Avon Church as the frontispiece for his first Illustrated Library Edition of 1899.

Mr. Sidney Lee is aware of the fact that Martin Droeshout was only fifteen years old when the Stratford actor died. But it is possible that he may not know that (in addition to the Shakespeare Mask which Droeshout drew for the frontispiece of the 1623 folio edition of the Plays of Shakespeare, in order to reveal, to those who were able to understand, the true facts of the Authorship of those plays), Martin Droeshout also drew frontispieces for other books, which may be similarly correctly characterised as cunningly composed, in order to reveal the true facts of the authorship of such works, unto those who were capable of grasping the hidden meaning of his engravings.

One other point it is worth while referring to. The question is frequently asked, if Bacon wrote under the name of Shakespeare, why so carefully conceal the fact? An answer is readily supplied by a little anecdote related by Ben Jonson, which was printed by the Shakespeare Society in 1842, in their "Notes of Ben Jonson's conversations with William Drummond of Hawthornden."

"He [Ben Jonson] was dilated by Sir James Murray to the King, for writting something against the Scots, in a play Eastward Hoe, and voluntarly imprissonned himself with Chapman and Marston who had written it amongst them. The report, was that they should then [have] had their ears cut and noses. After their delivery, he banqueted all his friends; there was Camden, Selden, and others; at the midst of the feast his old Mother dranke to him, and shew him a paper which she had (if the sentence had taken execution) to have mixed in the prisson among his drinke, which was full of lustie strong poison, and that she was no churle, she told, she was minded first to have drunk of it herself."

This was in 1605, and it is a strange and grim illustration of the dangers that beset men in the Highway of Letters.

It was necessary for Bacon to write under pseudonyms to conceal his identity, but he intended that at some time posterity should do him justice and it was for this purpose that, among the numerous clues he supplied to reveal himself he wrote "The Tempest" in its present form, which Emile Montégut writing in the *Revue des Deux Mondes* in 1865 declared to be the author's literary Testament.

The Island is the Stage. Prospero the prime Duke, the great Magician, represents the Mighty Author who says "my brother . . . called Anthonio who next thyself of all the world I lov'd" . . . . "graves at my command have wak'd their sleepers op'd and let them forth by my so potent Art" . . .

"and deeper than ever plummet sound
Ile drown my booke."

Yet he does not forget finally to add "I do . . . . require my Dukedome of thee, which perforce I know thou must restore."

The falsely crowned and gilded king of the Island who had stolen the wine (the poetry) "where should they find this grand liquor that hath gilded them" and whose name is Stephanos (Greek for crown) throws off at the close of the play, his false crown while Caliban says "What a thrice double asse was I to take this drunkard for a God."

The mighty Magician Prospero says "knowing I lov'd my bookes, he furnished me from mine own Library, with volumes, that I prize above my Dukedome." Bacon when he was dismissed from his high offices, devoted himself to his books. Not a book of any kind was found at New Place, Stratford.

Bacon's brother "whom next himself he loved" was called Anthony. "Gentle" Shakespeare of Stratford died from the effects of a "Drunken" bout!

It does matter whether it is thought that the immortal works were written by the sordid money-lender of Stratford, the "Swine without a head, without braine, wit, anything indeed, Ramping to Gentilitie"; or were written by him who was himself the "Greatest Birth of Time"; the man pre-eminently distinguished amongst the sons of earth; the man who in order to "do good to all mankind," disguised his personality "in a despised weed," and wrote under the name of William Shakespeare.

It does matter, and England is now declining any longer to *dishonour* and *defame* the greatest Genius of all time by continuing to identify him with the mean, drunken, ignorant, and absolutely unlettered, rustic of Stratford who never in his life wrote so much as his own name and in all probability was totally unable to read one single line of print.

The hour has come for revealing the truth. The hour has come when it is no longer necessary or desirable that the world should remain in ignorance that the Great Author of Shakespeare's Plays was himself alive when the Folio was published in 1623. The hour has come when all should know that this the greatest book produced by man was given to the world more carefully edited by its author as to every word in every column, as to every italic in every column, as to every apparent misprint in every column, than any book had ever before been edited, and more exactly printed than there seems any reasonable probability that any book will ever again be printed that may be issued in the future.

The hour has come when it is desirable and necessary to state with the utmost distinctness that

BACON IS SHAKESPEARE.

CHAPTER X.

Bacon is Shakespeare.

Proved mechanically in a short chapter on the long word Honorificabilitudinitatibus.

THE long word found in "Loves Labour's lost" was not created by the author of Shakespeare's plays. Mr. Paget Toynbee, writing in the *Athenæum* (London weekly) of December 2nd 1899, tells us the history of this long word.

It is believed to have first appeared in the Latin Dictionary by Uguccione, called "Magnæ Derivationes," which was written before the invention of printing, in the latter half of the twelfth century and seems never to have been printed. Excerpts from it were, however, included in the "Catholicon" of Giovanni da Genova, which was printed among the earliest of printed books (that is, it falls into the class of books known as "incunabula," so called because they belong to the "cradle of printing," the fifteenth century).

Plate XX.

Reduced Facsimile of Page 136 of the Shakespeare Folio, 1623.

Curat. A most singular and choise Epithat,

Draw out his Table-booke.

Peda. He draweth out the thred of his verbositie, finer then the staple of his argument. I abhor such phanaticall phantasims, such insociable and poynt deuise companions, such rackers of ortagriphie, as to speake dout fine, when he should say doubt; det, when he shold pronounce debt; d e b t, not det: he clepeth a Calf, Caufe: halfe, haufe: neighbour *vocatur* nebour; neigh abreuiated ne: this is abhominable, which he would call abhominable: it insinuateth me of infamie: *ne inteligis domine*, to make franticke, lunaticke?

Cura. *Laus deo, bene intelligo.*

Peda. *Bome boon for boon prescian*, a little scratcht, 'twil serue.

Enter Bragart, Boy.

Curat. *Vides ne quis venit*?

Peda. *Video, & gaudio.*

Brag. Chirra.

Peda. *Quari* Chirra, not Sirra?

Brag. Men of peace well incountred.

Ped. Most millitarie sir salutation

Boy. They haue beene at a great feast of Languages, and stolne the scraps.

Clow. O they haue liu'd long on the almes-basket of words. I maruell thy M. hath not eaten thee for a word, for thou art not so long by the head as honorificabilitudinitatibus: Thou art easier swallowed then a flapdragon.

Page. Peace, the peale begins.

Brag. Mounsier, are you not lettred?

Page. Yes, yes, he teaches boyes the Horne-booke: What is Ab speld backward with the horn on his head?

Peda. Ba, *puericia* with a horne added.

Pag. Ba most seely Sheepe, with a horne: you heare his learning.

Peda. *Quis quis*, thou Consonant?

Pag. The last of the fiue Vowels if You repeat them, or the fift if I.

Peda. I will repeat them: a e I.

Pag. The Sheepe, the other two concludes it o u.

Brag. Now by the salt waue of the mediteranium, a sweet tutch, a quicke vene we of wit, snip snap, quick & home, it reioyceth my intellect, true wit.

Page. Offered by a childe to an olde man: which is wit-old.

Peda. What is the figure? What is the figure?

Page. Hornes.

Peda. Thou disputes like an Infant: goe whip thy Gigge.

Pag. Lend me your Horne to make one, and I will whip about your Infamie *vnum cita* a gigge of a Cuckolds horne.

Clow. And I had but one penny in the world, thou shouldst haue it to buy Ginger bread: Hold, there is the very Remuneration I had of thy Maister, thou halfpenny purse of wit, thou Pidgeon-egge of discretion. O & the heauens were so pleased, that thou wert but my Bastard; What a ioyfull father wouldst thou make mee? Goe to, thou hast it *ad dungil*, at the fingers ends, as they say.

Peda. Oh I smell false Latine, *dunghel* for *vnguem*.

Brag. *Arts-man preambulat*, we will bee singled from the barbarous. Do you not educate youth at the Chargghouse on the top of the Mountaine?

Peda. Or *Mons* the hill.

Brag. At your sweet pleasure, for the Mountaine.

Peda. I doe *sans question*.

Bra. Sir, it is the Kings most sweet pleasure and affection, to congratulate the Princesse at her Pauilion, in the *posteriors* of this day, which the rude multitude call the after-noone.

Ped. The *posterior* of the day, most generous sir, is liable, congruent, and measurable for the after-noone: the word is well culd, chose, sweet, and apt I doe assure you sir, I doe assure.

Brag. Sir, the King is a noble Gentleman, and my familiar, I doe assure ye very good friend: for what is inward betweene vs, let it passe. I doe beseech thee remember thy curtesie. I beseech thee apparell thy head: and among other importunate & most serious designes, and of great import indeed too: but let that passe, for I must tell thee it will please his Grace (by the world) sometime to leane vpon my poore shoulder, and with his royall finger thus dallie with my excrement, with my mustachio: but sweet heart let that passe. By the world I recount no fable, some certaine speciall honours it pleaseth his greatnesse to impart to *Armado* a Souldier, a man of trauell, that hath seene the world: but let that passe; the very all of all is: but sweet heart, I do implore secrecie, that the King would haue mee present the Princesse (sweet chucke) with some delightfull ostentation, or show, or pageant, or anticke, or fire-worke: Now, vnderstanding that the Curate and your sweet self are good at such eruptions, and sodaine breaking out of myrth (as it were) I haue acquainted you withall, to the end to craue your assistance.

Peda. Sir, you shall present before her the Nine Worthies. Sir *Holofernes*, as concerning some entertainment of time, some show in the posterior of this day, to bee rendred by our assistants the Kings command: and this most gallant, illustrate and learned Gentleman, before the Princesse: I say none so fit as to present the Nine Worthies.

Curat. Where will you finde men worthy enough to present them?

Peda. *Iosua*, your selfe: my selfe, and this gallant gentleman *Iudas Machabeus*; this Swaine (because of his great limme or ioynt) shall passe *Pompey* the great, the Page *Hercules*.

Brag. Pardon sir, error: He is not quantitie enough for that Worthies thumb, hee is not so big as the end of his Club.

Peda. Shall I haue audience? he shall present *Hercules* in minoritie: his *enter* and *exit* shall bee strangling a Snake; and I will haue an Apologie for that purpose.

Pag. An excellent deuice: so if any of the audience hisse, you may cry, Well done *Hercules*, now thou crushest the Snake; that is the way to make an offence gracious, though few haue the grace to doe it.

Brag. For the rest of the Worthies?

Peda. I will play three my selfe.

Pag. Thrice worthy Gentleman.

Brag. Shall I tell you a thing?

Peda. We attend.

Brag. We will haue, if this fadge not, an Antique. I beseech you follow.

Ped. *Via* good-man *Dull*, thou hast spoken no word all this while.

Dull. Nor vnderstood none neither sir.

Ped. Alone, we will employ thee.

Dull. Ile make one in a dance, or so: or I will play on

Plate XX.

Reduced Facsimile of Page 136 of the Shakespeare Folio, 1623.

Text	Number of words in line in ordinary type.
Curat. A moſt ſingular and choiſe Epithat,	6
Draw out his Table-booke.	=
Peda. He draweth out the thred of his verboſitie, fi-	9
ner then the ſtaple of his argument. I abhor ſuch pha-	10
naticall phantaſims, ſuch inſociable and poynt deuiſe	6
companions, ſuch rackers of ortagriphie, as to ſpeake	8
dout fine, when he ſhould ſay doubt; det, when he ſhold	11
pronounce debt; d e b t, not det: he clepeth a Calf, Cauſe:	13
halfe, hauſe: neighbour *vocatur* nebour; neigh abreuiated	6
ne: this is abhominable, which he would call abhomi-	9
nable: it inſinuateth me of inſamie: *ne inteligis domine*, to	6
make franticke, lunaticke?	3
Cura. Laus deo, bene intelligo.	=
Peda. Bome boon for boon preſcian, a little ſcratcht, 'twil	4
ſerue.	1
Enter Bragart, Boy.	=
Curat. Vides ne quis venit?	=
Peda. Video, & gaudio.	=
Brag. Chirra.	1
Peda. Quari Chirra, not Sirra?	3
Brag. Men of peace well incountred.	5
Ped. Moſt millitarie ſir ſalutation	4
Boy. They haue beene at a great feaſt of Languages,	9
and ſtolne the ſcraps.	4
Clow. O they haue liu'd long on the almes-basket of	10
words. I maruell thy M. hath not eaten thee for a word,	12
for thou art not ſo long by the head as honorificabilitu-	11
dinitatibus: Thou art eaſier ſwallowed then a flapdra-	151
gon.	
Page. Peace, the peale begins.	
Brag. Mounſier, are you not lettred?	
Page. Yes, yes, he teaches boyes the Horne-booke:	
What is Ab ſpeld backward with the horn on his head?	
Peda. Ba, *puericia* with a horne added.	
Pag. Ba moſt ſeely Sheepe, with a horne: you heare	
his learning.	

Plate XXI.

PORTION OF PAGE 136, FULL SIZE, AS IN THE SHAKESPEARE FOLIO, 1623.

Plate XXI.

Portion of Page 136, full size, as in the Shakespeare Folio, 1623.

In this "Catholicon," which, though undated, was printed before A.D. 1500, we read

"Ab *honorifico, hic* et *hec honorificabilis,—le* et *hec honororificabilitas,—tis* et *hec honorificabilitudinitas,* et est longissima dictio, que illo versu continetur—

Fulget Honorificabilitudinitatibus iste."

It is perhaps not without interest to call the reader's attention to the fact that "Fulget hon | orifi | cabili | tudini | tatibus | iste" forms a neat Latin hexameter. It will be found that the revelation derived from the long word Honorificabilitudinitatibus is itself also in the form of a Latin hexameter.

The long word Honorificabilitudinitatibus occurs in the Quarto edition of "Loues Labor's Lost," which is stated to be "Newly corrected and augmented by W. Shakespere." Imprinted in London by W. W. for Cutbert Burby. 1598.

This is the very first play that bore the name W. Shakespere, but so soon as he had attached the name W. Shakespere to that play, the great author Francis Bacon caused to be issued almost immediately a book attributed to Francis Meres which is called "Palladis Tamia, Wits Treasury" and is stated to be Printed by P. Short for Cuthbert Burbie, 1598. This is the same publisher as the publisher of the Quarto of "Loues Labor's lost" although both the Christian name and the surname are differently spelled.

This little book "Palladis Tamia, Wits Treasury" tells us on page 281, "As Plautus and Seneca are "accounted the best for comedy and tragedy among "the Latines, so Shakespeare among ye English, "is the most excellent in both kinds for the stage; "for Comedy, witness his Getleme of Verona, his "Errors, his Love Labors lost, his Love Labours "wonne, his Midsummers night dreame, and his "Merchant of Venice: for Tragedy, his Richard the 2, "Richard the 3, Henry the 4, King John, Titus "Andronicus, and his Romeo and Juliet."

Here we are distinctly told that eleven other plays are also Shakespeare's work although only Loues Labors lost at that time bore his name.

We refer on page 138 to the reason why it had become absolutely necessary for the Author to affix a false name to all these twelve plays. For our present purpose it is sufficient to point out that on the very first occasion when the name W. Shakespere was attached to any play, viz., to the play called "Loues Labor's lost," the Author took pains to insert a revelation that would enable him to claim his own when the proper time should arrive. Accordingly he prepared the page which is found F 4 (the little book is not paged) in the Quarto of "Loues Labor's lost" which was published in 1598. A photo-facsimile of the page is shewn, Page 105, Plate 22.

So far as is known there never was any other edition printed until the play appeared in the Folio of 1623 under the name of "Loues Labour's lost," and we put before the reader a reduced facsimile of the whole page 136 of the 1623 Folio, on which the long word occurs, Page 86, Plate 20, and we give also an exact full size photo reproduction of a portion of the first column of that page, Page 87, Plate 21.

On comparing the page of the Quarto with that of the Folio, it will be seen that the Folio page commences with the same word as does the Quarto and that each and every word, and each and every italic in the Folio is exactly reproduced from the Quarto excepting that Alms-basket in the Folio is printed with a hyphen to make it into two words. A hyphen is also inserted in the long word as it extends over one line to the next. The only other change is that the lines are a little differently arranged. These slight differences are by no means accidental, because Alms-basket is hyphened to count as two words and thereby cause the long word to be the 151st word. This is exceedingly important and it was only by a misprint in the Quarto that it incorrectly appears there as the 150th word. By the rearrangement of the lines, the long word appears on the 27th line, and the line, "What is A.B. speld backward with the horn on his head" appears as it should do on the 33rd line. At the time the Quarto was issued, when the trouble was to get Shakespere's name attached to the plays, these slight printer's errors in the Quarto—for they are printer's errors—were of small consequence, but when the play was reprinted in the Folio of 1623 all these little blemishes were most carefully corrected.

The long word Honorificabilitudinitatibus is found in "Loues Labour's lost" not far from the commencement of the Fifth Act, which is called Actus Quartus in the 1623 folio, and on Page 87, Plate 21, is given a full size photo facsimile from the folio, of that portion of page 136, in which the word occurs in the 27th line.

On lines 14, 15 occurs the phrase, "Bome boon for boon prescian, a little scratcht, 'twil serve." I do not know that hitherto any rational explanation has been given of the reason why this reference to the pedantic grammarian "Priscian" is there inserted.

The mention of Priscian's name can have no possible reference to anything apparent in the text, but it refers solely and entirely to the phrase which is to be formed by the transposition of the twenty-seven letters contained in the long word Honorificabilitudinitatibus; and it was absolutely impossible that the citation of Priscian could ever have been understood before the sentence containing the information which is of the most important description had been "revealed." We say "revealed" because the riddle could never have been "guessed."

The "revealed" and "all revealing" sentence forms a correct Latin hexameter, and we will proceed to prove that it is without possibility of doubt or question the real solution which the "Author" intended to be known at some future time, when he placed the long word Honorificabilitudinitatibus, which is composed of twenty-seven letters, on the twenty-seventh line of page 136, where it appears as the 151st word printed in ordinary type.

The all-important statement which reveals the

authorship of the plays in the most clear and direct manner (every one of the twenty-seven letters composing the long word being employed and no others) is in the form of a correct Latin hexameter, which reads as follows—

HI	LUDI	F. BACONIS	NATI	TUITI	ORBI
These plays		F. Bacon's	offspring	are preserved	for the world.

This verse will scan as a spondaic hexameter as under

HĪ LŪ | DĪ F̄ | B̄ACŌ | NĪS NĀ | TĪ TŬĬ | T̄Ī ORBĪ

HI One long syllable meaning "these."

LUDI Two long syllables meaning "stage plays," and especially "stage plays" in contradistinction to "Circus games." (Suetonius Hist: Julius Caes: 10. Venationes autem Ludosque et cum collega et separatim edidit).

F, One long syllable. Now for the first time can the world be informed why the sneer "Bome boon for boon prescian, a little scratcht, 'twil serve" was inserted on lines 14, 15, page 136 of the folio of 1623. Priscian declares that F was a mute and Bacon mocks him for so doing. Ausonius while giving the pronunciation of most letters of the alphabet does not afford us any information respecting the sound of F, but Quintilian xii. 10, s. 29, describes the pronunciation of the Roman F. Some scholars understand him as indicating that the Roman F had rather a rougher sound than the English F. Others agree with Dr. H. J. Roby, and are of opinion that Quintilian means that the Roman F was "blown out between the intervals of the teeth with no sound of voice." (See Roby's Grammar of the Latin language, 1881, xxxvi.) But Dr. A. Bos in his "Petit Traité de prononciation Latine," 1897, asserts that the old Latin manner of pronouncing F was effé. Even if Dr. A. Bos is correct it is not at all likely that effé was a dissyllable, but most probably it would be sounded very nearly like the Greek "φι," that is as "pfé." In any case (even if it were a dissyllable) F would, with the DI of LUDI, form two long syllables and scan as a spondee. The use of single consonants to form long or short syllables was very common among the Romans, but such appear mostly in lines impossible to quote.

But the Great Author was well acquainted with such instances, and in this same page 136, in lines 6, 7, 8, he gives an example, shewing that the letter "B," although silent in debt, becomes, when debt is spelled, one of the four full words—d e b t, each of which has to be counted to make up the number "151."*

---

* Under what is now known as "Rask's law" the Roman F becomes B in the Teutonic languages: fero, bear; frater, brother; feru, brew; flo, blow, etc., etc., shewing that the Roman F was by no means really a mute.

This, which is an example of the great value and importance of what, in many of the plays, appears to be merely "silly talk" affords a strong additional evidence of the correctness of the "revealed" and "revealing" sentence which we shew was intended by the author to be constructed out of the long word. Bacon therefore was amply justified in making use of F as a long syllable to form the second half of a spondee.

BACONIS Three long syllables, the final syllable being long by position. Pedantic grammarians might argue that natus being a participle ought not to govern a genitive case, but should be followed by a preposition with the ablative case, and that we ought to say "e Bacone nati" or "de Bacone nati." Other pedants have declared that natus is properly, i.e., classically, said of the mother only, although in low Latin, such as the Vulgate, we find 1 John v. 2, "Natos Dei," "born of God." But the Author of the plays, who instead of having "small Latin and less Greek" knew "*All* Latin and very much Greek," was well aware that Vergil, Aeneid i. 654 (or 658 when the four additional lines are inserted at the beginning) gives us "Maxima natarum Priami," "greatest of the daughters of Priam," and in Aeneid ii. 527 "Unus natorum

Priami," "one of the sons of Priam." There exists therefore the highest classical authority for the use of "Nati" in the sense of "Sons" or "offspring" governing a genitive case. "F. Baconis nati," "Francis Bacon's offspring," is therefore absolutely and classically correct.

NATI Two long syllables. A noun substantive meaning as shewn above "sons" or "offspring."

TUITI Two short syllables and one long syllable, which last is elided and disappears before the "o" of orbi. Tuiti which is the same word as tuti is a passive past participle meaning saved or preserved. It is derived from tueor, which is generally used as a deponent or reflexive verb, but tueor is used by Varro and the legal writers as a passive verb.

ORBI Two long syllables. The word orbi may be either the plural nominative of orbus meaning "deprived" "orphaned," or it may be the dative singular of Orbis meaning "for the world." Both translations make good sense because the plays are "preserved for the world" and are "preserved orphaned." The present writer prefers the translation "for the world," indeed he thinks that to most classical scholars "tuiti orbi," "preserved bereft," looks almost like a contradiction in terms.

Now and now only can a reasonable explanation be given for the first time of the purpose of the reference to Priscian, in lines 14 and 15, Plate 21, Page 87. And it is a singular circumstance that so far as the writer is aware not one of the critics has perceived that the mockery of Priscian forms a neat English iambic hexameter, indeed, in almost all modern editions of the Shakespeare plays, both the form and the meaning of the line have been utterly destroyed. In the original the line reads "Bome boon for boon prescian, a little scracht, 'twil serve."

Perhaps the reader will be enabled better to understand the sneer and the mockery by reading the following couplet—

A fíg for óld Priscián, a líttle scrátcht, 'twil sérve
A póet súrely néed not áll his rúles obsérve.

And we still more perfectly understand the purpose of the hexameter form of the reference to Priscian if we scan the line side by side with the "revealed" interpretation of the long word honorificabilitudinitatibus.

Bome boon	for boon	prescian	a lit	tle scratcht	'twil serve
HI LU	DI F	BACO	NIS NA	TI TUI	TI ORBI

These plays F Bacon's offspring are preserved for the world.

This explanation of the real meaning to be derived from the long word honorificabilitudinitatibus seems to be so convincing as scarcely to require further proof. But the Author of the plays intended when the time had fully come for him to claim his own that there should not be any possibility of cavil or doubt. He therefore so arranged the plays and the acts of the plays in the folio of 1623 that the long word should appear upon the 136th page, be the 151st word thereon, should fall on the 27th line and that the interpretation should indicate the numbers 136 and 151, thus forming a mechanical proof so positive that it can neither be misconstrued nor explained away, a mechanical proof that provides an evidence which absolutely compels belief.

The writer desires especially to bring home to the reader the manifest fact that the revealed and revealing sentence must have been constructed before the play of "Loues Labor's lost" first appeared in 1598, and that when the plays were printed in their present form in the 1623 folio the scenes and the acts of the preceding plays and the printing of the columns in all those plays as well as in the play of "Loues Labour's lost" required to be arranged with extraordinary skill in order that the revealing page in the 1623 folio should commence with the first word of the revealing page in the original quarto of 1598, and that that page should form the 136th page of the folio, so that the long word "Honorificabilitudinitatibus" should appear on page 136, be the 151st word, and fall upon the 27th line.

Bacon tells us that there are 24 letters in the alphabet (*i* and *j* being deemed to be forms of the same letter, as are also *u* and *v*). Bacon was himself accustomed frequently to use the letters of the alphabet as numerals (the Greeks similarly used letters for numerals). Thus A is 1, B is 2 . . . Y is 23, Z is 24. Let us take as an example Bacon's own name—B=2, a=1, c=3, o=14, n=13; all these added together make the number 33, a number about which it is possibly to say a good deal.* We now put the numerical value to each of the letters that form the long word, and we shall find that their total amounts to the number 287, thus:

H O N O R I F I C A B I L I T U
8 14 13 14 17 9 6 9 3 1 2 9 11 9 19 20
D I N I T A T I B U S
4 9 13 9 19 1 19 9 2 20 18=287

From a word containing so large a number of letters as twenty-seven it is evident that we can construct very numerous words and phrases; but I think it "surpasses the wit of man" to construct any "sentence" other than the "revealed sentence," which by its construction shall reveal not only the number of the page on which it appears—which is 136—but shall also reveal the fact that the long word shall be the 151st word printed in ordinary type counting from the first word.

On one side of the facsimile reproduction of part of page 136 of the 1623 folio, numbers are placed shewing

* See Page 104.

that the long word is on the 27th line, which was a skilfully purposed arrangement, because there are 27 letters in the word. There is also another set of numbers at the other side of the facsimile page which shews that, counting from the first word, the long word is the 151st word. How is it possible that the revealing sentence, "Hi ludi F. Baconis nati tuiti orbi," can tell us that the page is 136 and the position of the long word is the 151st word? The answer is simple. The numerical value of the initial letters and of the terminal letters of the revealed sentence, when added together, give us 136, the number of the page, while the numerical value of all the other letters amount to the number 151, which is the number of words necessary to find the position of the long word "Honorificabilitudinitatibus," which is the 151st word on page 136, counting those printed in ordinary type, the italic words being of course omitted.

The solution is as follows

HI
LUDI
F
BACONIS
NATI
TUITI
ORBI

the initial letters of which are

H L F B N T O

their numerical values being

8 11 6 2 13 19 14=total 73

and the terminal letters are

I I S I I I

their numerical values being

9 9 18 9 9 9 = total 63

Adding this 63 **to** 73 **we get** 136

while the intermediate letters are

U D A C O N I A T U I T R B

their numerical values being

20 4 1 3 14 13 9 1 19 20 9 19 17 2 = 151

Total 287

The reader thus sees that it is a fact that in the "revealed" sentence the sum of the numerical values of the initial letters, when added to the sum of the numerical values of the terminal letters, do, with mathematical certainty produce 136, the number of the page in the first folio, which is 136, and that the sum of the numerical values of the intermediate letters amounts to 151, which gives the position of the long word on that page, which is the 151st word in ordinary type. These two sums of 136 and 151, when added together, give 287, which is the sum of the numerical value of all the letters of the long word "Honorificabilitudinitatibus," which, as we saw on page 99, amounted to the same total, 287.

As a further evidence of the marvellous manner in which the Author had arranged the whole plan, the long word of 27 letters is placed on the 27th line.

Can anyone be found who will pretend to produce from the 27 letters which form the word "Honorificabilitudinitatibus" another sentence which shall also tell the number of the page, 136, and that the position of the long word on the page is the 151st word?

I repeat that to do this "surpasses the wit of man," and that therefore the true solution of the meaning of the long word "Honorificabilitudinitatibus," about which so much nonsense has been written, is without possibility of doubt or question to be found by arranging the letters to form the Latin hexameter.

HI LUDI F. BACONIS NATI TUITI ORBI

These plays F. Bacon's offspring are preserved for the world.

It is not possible to afford a clearer mechanical proof that

THE SHAKESPEARE PLAYS ARE BACON'S OFFSPRING.

It is not possible to make a clearer and more definite statement that

BACON IS THE AUTHOR OF THE PLAYS.

It is not possible that any doubt can any longer be entertained respecting the manifest fact that

BACON IS SHAKESPEARE.

CHAPTER XI.

On the revealing page 136 in "Loves Labour's lost."

In the previous chapter it was pointed out that using letters for numbers, Bacon's name is represented by 33.

B A C O N .
2 1 3 14 13 = 33

and that the long word possesses the numerical value of 287.

H O N O R I F I C A B I L I T U
8 14 13 14 17 9 6 9 3 1 2 9 11 9 19 20
D I N I T A T I B U S
4 9 13 9 19 1 19 9 2 20 18 = 287

In the Shakespeare folio, Page 136, shewn in Plate 20 and Plate 21, on Pages 86-7, ON LINE 33, we read "What is Ab speld backward with the horn on his head?"

The answer which is given is evidently an incorrect answer, it is "Ba, puericia with a horne added," and the Boy mocks him with "Ba most seely sheepe, with a horne: you heare his learning."

The reply should of course have been in Latin. The Latin for a horn is cornu. The real answer therefore is "Ba corn-u fool."

This is the exact answer you might expect to find on the line 33, since the number 33 indicates Bacon's name. And now, and now only, can be explained the very frequent use of the ornament representing a Horned Sheep, inside and outside "Baconian" books, under whatever name they may be known. An example will be found at the head of the present chapter on page 103. The uninitiated are still "informed" or rather "misinformed" that this ornament alludes to the celebrated Golden Fleece of the Argonauts and they little suspect that they have been purposely fooled, and that the real reference is to Bacon.

It should be noted here that in the Quarto of "Loues Labor's lost," see Plate 22, Page 105, if the heading "Loues Labor's lost" be counted as a line, we read on the 33rd line: "Ba most seely sheepe with a horne: you heare his learning." This would direct you to a reference to Bacon, although not so perfectly as the final arrangement in the folio of 1623.

Proceeding with the other lines in the page, we read:—

"Quis quis, thou consonant?"

This means "Who, who"? [which Bacon] because in order to make the revelation complete we must be told that it is "Francis" Bacon, so as to leave no ambiguity or possibility of mistake. How then is it possible that we can be told that it is Francis Bacon? We read in answer to the question:

Curat. A most singuler and choyce Epithat,

Draw-out his Table-booke.

Peda. He draweth out the thred of his verbositie, finer then the staple of his argument. I abhorre such phanatticall phantasims, such insociable and poynt deuise companions, such rackers of ortagriphie, as to speake dout fine, when he should say doubt; det, when he shold pronounce debt; d e b t, not det: he clepeth a Calfe, Caufe: halfe, haufe: neighbour *vocatur* nebour; neigh abreuiated ne: this is abhominable, which he would call abbominable, it insinuateth me of infamie: *ne inteligis domine*, to make frantique lunatique?

Curat. Laus deo, bene intelligo.

Peda. Bome boon for boon prescian, a litle scratcht, twil serue.

Enter Bragart, Boy.

Curat. Vides ne quis venit?

Peda. Video, et gaudio.

Brag. Chirra.

Peda. Quari Chirra, not Sirra?

Brag. Men of peace well incontred.

Ped. Most millitarie sir salutation.

Boy. They haue been at a great feast of Languages, and stolne the scraps.

Clow. O they haue lyud long on the almsbasket of wordes. I maruaile thy M. hath not eaten thee for a worde, for thou art not so long by the head as honorificabilitudinitatibus: Thou art easier swallowed then a flapdragon.

Page. Peace, the peale begins.

Brag. Mounsier, are you not lettred?

Page. Yes yes, he teaches boyes the Horne-booke: What is Ab speld backward with the horne on his head?

Peda. Ba, *puericia* with a horne added,

Pag. Ba most seely Sheepe, with a horne: you heare his (learning.

Peda. Quis quis thou Consonant?

Pag. The last of the fiue Vowels if You repeate them, or the fift if I.

Peda. I will repeate them: a e I.

Pag. The Sheepe, the other two concludes it o u.

Brag. Now by the sault wane of the meditaranium, a sweete

Plate XXII.

FACSIMILE FROM "LOUES LABOR'S LOST," FIRST EDITION, 1598.

Plate XXII.

Facsimile from "Loues Labor's Lost," first edition, 1598.

"Quis quis, thou consonant?
The last of five vowels if you repeat them, the fifth if I.
I will repeat them a, e, I.
The Sheepe, the other two concludes it o, u."

Now here we are told that a, e, I, o, u is the answer to Quis quis, and we must note that the I is a capital letter. Therefore a is followed by e, but I being a capital letter does not follow e but starts afresh, and we must read I followed by o, and o followed by u.

this 6th of June. 1595.
yor Lopp in all humblenes to
be Commanded.
Fra: Bacon

Plate XXIII.

FACSIMILE OF A CONTEMPORARY COPY OF A LETTER OF FRANCIS BACON.

Is it possible that these vowels will give us the Christian name of Bacon? Can it be that we are told on what page to look? The answer to both these questions is the affirmative "Yes."

The great Folio of Shakespeare was published in 1623, and in the following year, 1624, there was brought out a great Cryptographic book by the "Man in the

Moon." We shall speak about this work presently; suffice for the moment to say that this book was issued as the key to the Shakespeare Folio of 1623. If we turn to page 254 in the Cryptographic book we shall find Chapter XIV. "De Transpositione

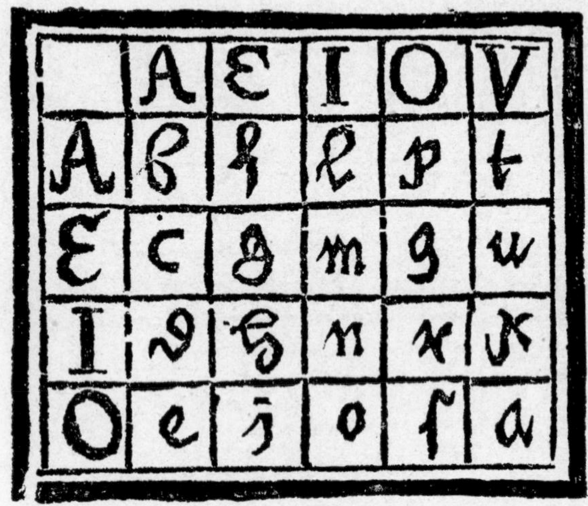

	A	E	I	O	V
A	b	f	l	p	t
E	c	g	m	q	u
I	d	h	n	r	x
O	e	j	o	ſ	a

Quarta Tabula, ex Vigenerio, pag. 202. b. *vindicat ſibi præcipuum, quod Vocalibus tantùm ſcribere hîc liceat.*

Plate XXIV.

FACSIMILES FROM PAGE 255 OF "GUSTAVI SELENI CRYPTOMENYTICES," PUBLISHED 1624.

[The Square Table is much enlarged].

Obliquâ, per dispositionem Alphabeti." This chapter describes how, by means of square tables, one letter followed by another letter will give the cypher letter. On the present page appears the square, which is shown in Plate 24, which enables us to answer the question "Quis quis."

By means of this square we perceive that "a" followed by "e" gives us the letter F, that "I" followed by "o" gives us the letter R, and that "o" followed by "u" gives us the letter A. The answer therefore to Quis quis (which Bacon do you mean) is Fra [Bacon]. *See* Plate 23, Page 107.

But what should induce us to look at this particular chapter on page 254 of the Cryptographic book for the

	A	*E*	*I*	*O*	*V*
A	b	f	l	p	t
E	c	g	m	q	u
I	d	h	n	r	x
O	e	i	o	s	a

Plate XXV.

FACSIMILE FROM PAGE 202b OF "TRAICTÉ DES CHIFFRES OU SECRÈTES MANIÈRES D'ESCRIRE," PAR VIGENÈRE.

solution? The answer is clearly given in the wonderful page 136 of the 1623 Folio of Shakespeare.

As has been pointed out the numerical value of the long word Honorificabilitudinitatibus is 287, and the numerical value of Bacon is 33. We have found Bacon from Ba with a horn, and we require the remainder of his name, accordingly deduct 33 from 287, and we get the answer 254 which is the number of the required page in the Cryptographic book of 1624. But the wise Author knew that someone would say "How does this apply to the 1598 Quarto published twenty-six years before the great Cryptographic book appeared?" On Plate 24, Page 108, taken from page 255 of the Cryptographic book of 1624, it is shewn that the following lines are attached to the square

"Quarta Tabula, ex Vigenerio, pag. 202.b, etc."
= Square table taken from Vigenerio, page 202.b.

This reference is to the work entitled, "Traicté des chiffres ou secrètes manières d'escrire": par Blaise de Vigenère, which was published in Paris in 1586. Spedding states (Vol. I. of "Bacon's Letters and Life," p. 6-8) that Francis Bacon went in 1576 to France, with Sir Amias Paulet, the English Ambassador. Bacon remained in France until 1578-9, and when in 1623 he published his "De Augmentis Scientiarum"—(the Advancement of Learning) he tells us that while in Paris he invented his own method of secret writing. *See* Spedding's "Works of Bacon," Vol. 4, p. 445.

The system which Bacon then invented is now known as the Biliteral Cypher, and it is in fact practically the same as that which is universally employed in Telegraphy under the name of the Morse Code.

A copy of Vigenère's book will be found in the present writer's Baconian library, for he knew by the ornaments and by the other marks that Bacon must have had a hand in its production.

Anyone, therefore, reading the Quarto edition of "Loues Labor's lost," 1598, and putting *two* and *two* together will find on p. 202.b of Vigenère's book, the Table, of which a facsimile is here given, Plate 25, Page 109. This square is even more clear than the square table in the great Cryptographic book.

Thus, upon the same page 136 in the Folio, or on F. 4 in the Quarto, in addition to Honorificabilitudinitatibus containing the revealing sentence "Hi ludi F Baconis nati tuiti orbi"="These plays F Bacon's offspring are entrusted to the world," we see that we are able to discover on line 33 the name of Bacon, and by means of the lines which follow that it is Fra. Bacon who is referred to.

Before parting with this subject we will give one or two examples to indicate how often the number 33 is employed to indicate Bacon.

We have just shewn that on page 136 of the Folio we obtain Bacon's name on line 33. On page 41 we refer to Ben Jonson's "Every man out of his Humour." In an extremely rare early Quarto [*circa* 1600] of that play some unknown hand has numbered the pages referring to Sogliardo (Shakespeare) and Puntarvolo (Bacon) 32 and 32 repeated. Incorrect pagination is a common method used in "revealing" books to call attention to some statements, and anyone can perceive that the second 32 is really 33 and as usual reveals something about Bacon.

On page 61 we point out that on page 33 of the little book called "The Great Assizes holden in Parnassus" Apollo speaks. As the King speaks in a Law Court only through the mouth of his High Chancellor so

Apollo speaks in the supposititious law action through the mouth of his Chancellor of Parnassus, who is Lord Verulam, i.e. Bacon. Thus again Bacon is found on page 33. The writer could give very numerous examples, but these three which occur incidentally will give some idea how frequently the number 33 is used to indicate Bacon.*

The whole page 136 of the Folio is cryptographic, but we will not now proceed to consider any other matters contained upon it, but pass on to discuss the great Cryptographic book which was issued under Bacon's instructions in the year following the publication of the great Folio of Shakespeare. Before, however, speaking of the book, we must refer to the enormous pains always taken to provide traps for the uninitiated.

If you go to Lunæburg, where the Cryptographic book was published, you will be referred to the

---

*The number 33 too obviously represented Bacon, and therefore 53 which spells sow (S 18, O 14, W 21=53) was substituted for 33. Scores of examples can be found where on page 53 some reference is made to Bacon in books published under various names, especially in the Emblem Books. In many cases page 55 is *misprinted* as 53. In the Shakespeare Folio 1623 on the first page 53 we read "Hang Hog is latten for Bacon," and on the second page 53 we find "Gammon of Bacon." When the seven extra plays were added in the third folio 1664 in each of the two new pages 53 appears "St. Albans." In the fifth edition, published by Rowe in 1709, on page 53 we read "deeper than did ever Plummet sound I'll drown my Book"; and on page 55 *misprinted* 53 (the only mispagination in the whole book of 3324 pages) we find "I do . . . . require My Dukedom of thee, which perforce I know Thou must restore." In Bacon's "Advancement of Learning," first English edition, 1640, on page 55 *misprinted* 53 in the margin in capital letters (the only name in capital letters in the whole book) we read "BACON." In Florio's "Second Frutes," 1591, on page 53, is "slice of bacon" and also "gammon of bakon," to shew that Bacon may be misspelled as it is in Drayton's "Polyolbion," 1622, where on page 53 we find *Becanus*. A whole book could be filled with similar instances.

Library at Wolfenbüttel and to a series of letters to be found there which contain instructions to the engraver which seem to prove that this book has no possible reference to Shakespeare. We say, seem to prove, for the writer possesses accurate photographs of all these letters and they really prove exactly the reverse, for they are, to those capable of understanding them, cunningly devised false clues, quite clear and plain. That these letters are snares for the uninitiated,

Plate XXVI.

the writer, who possesses a "Baconian" library, could easily prove to any competent scholar.

Before referring to the wonderful title page of the Cryptographic book which reveals the Bacon-Shakespeare story, it is necessary to direct the reader's attention to Camden's "Remains," published 1616. We may conclude that Bacon had a hand in the production of this book, since Spedding's "Bacon's Works," Vol. 6, p. 351, and Letters, Vol. 4, p. 211, informs us that Bacon assisted Camden with his "Annales."

In Camden's "Remains," 1616, the Chapter on Surnames, p. 106, commences with an ornamental headline like the head of Chapter 10, p. 84, but printed "*upside down.*" A facsimile of the heading in Camden's book is shewn in Plate 26, page 113.

This trick of the upside down printing of ornaments and even of engravings is continually resorted to when some revelation concerning Bacon's works is given. Therefore in Camden's "Remains" of 1616 in the Chapter on Surnames, because the head ornament is printed upside down, we may be perfectly certain that we shall find some revelation concerning Bacon and Shakespeare.

Accordingly on p. 121 we find as the name of a village "Bacon Creping." There never was a village called "Bacon Creping." And on page 128 we read "such names as Shakespeare, Shotbolt, Wagstaffe." In referring to the great Cryptographic book, we shall realise the importance of this conjunction of names.

On Plate 27, Page 115, we give a reduced facsimile of the title page, which as the reader will see, states in Latin that the work is by Gustavus Selenus, and contains systems of Cryptographic writing, also methods of the shorthand of Trithemius. The Imprint at the end, under a very handsome example of the double A ornament which in various forms is used generally in books of Baconian learning, states that it was published and printed at Lunæburg in 1624. Gustavus Selenus we are told in the dedicatory poems prefixed to the work is "Homo lunæ" [the man in the Moon].

Look first at the whole title page; on the top is a

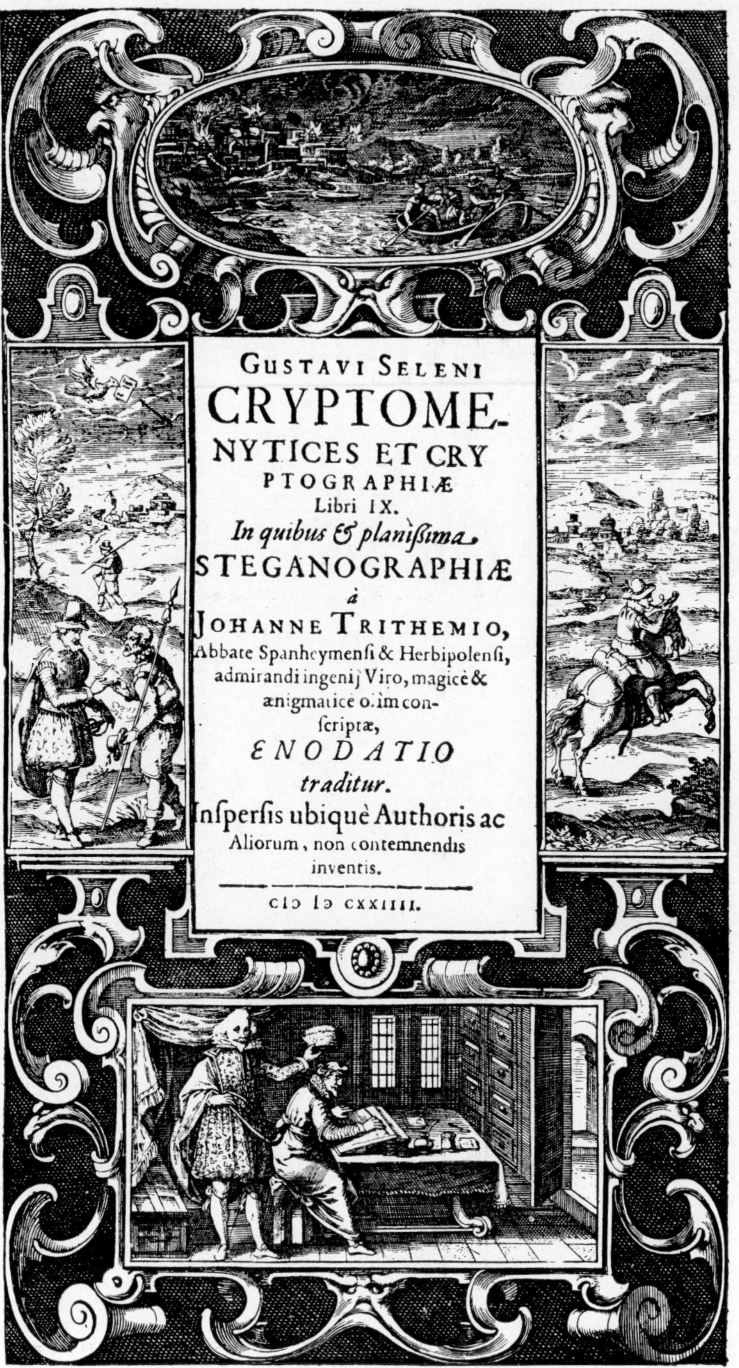

GUSTAVI SELENI

CRYPTOME-
NYTICES ET CRY
PTOGRAPHIÆ
Libri IX.

In quibus & planiſſima
STEGANOGRAPHIÆ
à
JOHANNE TRITHEMIO,
Abbate Spanheymenſi & Herbipolenſi,
admirandi ingenij Viro, magicè &
ænigmaticè olim con-
ſcriptæ,

ENODATIO
traditur.

Inſperſis ubiquè Authoris ac
Aliorum, non contemnendis
inventis.

CIϽ IϽ CXXIIII.

Plate XXVII.

FACSIMILE TITLE PAGE.

Plate XXVII.

FACSIMILE TITLE PAGE.

Plate XXVIII.

Left-Hand Portion, much enlarged, of Plate XXVII.

Plate XXVIII.

Left-Hand Portion, much enlarged, of Plate XXVII

Plate XXIX.

Right-Hand Portion, much enlarged, of Plate XXVII.

Plate XXIX.

Right-Hand Portion, much enlarged, of Plate XXVII.

Plate XXX.

Top Portion of Plate XXVII., much enlarged.

Plate XXX.

Top Portion of Plate XXVII., much enlarged.

Plate XXXI.

Bottom Portion of Plate XXVII., much enlarged.

Plate XXXI.

Bottom Portion of Plate XXVII., much enlarged.

tempest with flaming beacons, on the left (of the reader) is a gentleman giving something to a spearman, and there are also other figures; on the right is a man on horseback, and at the bottom in a square is a much dressed up man taking the "Cap of Maintenance" from a man writing a book.

Examine first the left-hand picture shewn enlarged, Plate 28, Page 118. You see a man, evidently Bacon, giving his writing to a Spearman who is dressed in actor's boots (see Stothard's painting of Falstaff in the "Merry Wives of Windsor" wearing similar actor's boots, Plate 32, Page 127). Note that the Spearman has a sprig of bay in the hat which he holds in his hand. This man is a Shake-Spear, nay he really is a correct portrait of the Stratford householder, which you will readily perceive if you turn to Dugdale's engraving of the Shakespeare bust, Plate 5, Page 14. In the middle distance the man still holding a spear, still being a Shake-Speare, walks with a staff, he is therefore a Wagstaffe. On his back are books— the books of the plays. In the sky is seen an arrow, no, it is not sufficiently long for an arrow, it is a Shotbolt (Shakespeare, Wagstaffe, Shotbolt, of Camden's "Remains"). This Shotbolt is near to a bird which seems about to give to it the scroll it carries in its beak. But is it a real bird? No, it has no real claws, its feet are Jove's lightnings, verily, "it is the Eagle of great verse."

Next, look on Plate 29, Page 119, which is the picture on the right of the title page. Here you see that the same Shake-spear whom we saw in the left-hand picture is now riding on a courser. That he is the same man is shewn by the sprig of bay in his hat, but he is no longer a Shake-spear, he is a Shake-*spur*. Note how much the artist has emphasised the drawing of the spur. It is made the one prominent thing in the whole picture. We refer our reader to "The Returne from Pernassus" (see pp. 47-48) where he will read,

> "England affordes those glorious vagabonds
> "That carried earst their fardels on their backes
> "Coursers to ride on through the gazing streetes."

Now glance at the top picture on the title page (see Plate 27, Page 115,) which is enlarged in Plate 30, Page 122. Note that the picture is enclosed in the magic circle of the imagination, surrounded by the masks of Tragedy, Comedy, and Farce (in the same way as Stothard's picture of the "Merry Wives of Windsor," Plate 32, Page 127). The engraving represents a tempest with beacon lights; No; it represents "The Tempest" of Shakespeare and tells you that the play is filled with Bacon lights. (In the sixteenth century Beacon was pronounced Bacon. "Bacon great Beacon of the State.")

We have already pointed out that "The Tempest," as Emile Montégut shewed in the *Revue des Deux Mondes* in 1865, is a mass of Bacon's revelations concerning himself.

At the bottom (see Plate 27, Page 115, and Plate 31 Page 123), within the "four square corners of fact,"

Plate XXXII.

Scene from "The Merry Wives of Windsor," painted by Thomas Stothard.

Plate XXXII.

Scene from "The Merry Wives of Windsor," painted by Thomas Stothard.

surrounded with disguised masks of Tragedy, Comedy, and Farce, is shewn the same man who gave the scroll to the Spearman, see Plate 29, Page 118 (note the pattern of his sleeves). He is now engaged in writing his book, while an Actor, very much overdressed and wearing a mask something like the accepted mask of Shakespeare, is lifting from the real writer's head a cap known in Heraldry as the "Cap of Maintenance." Again we refer to our quotation on page 48.

> "Those glorious vagabonds . . . . .
> Sooping it in their glaring Satten sutes."

Is not this masquerading fellow an actor "Sooping it in his glaring Satten sute"? The figure which we say represents Bacon, see Plate 28, wears his clothes as a gentleman. Nobody could for a moment imagine that the masked creature in Plate 31 was properly wearing his own clothes. No, he is "sooping it in his glaring Satten sute."

The whole title page clearly shows that it is drawn to give a revelation about Shakespeare, who might just as well have borne the name of Shotbolt or of Wagstaffe or of Shakespur, see "The Tempest," Act v., Scene 1.

> "The strong bass'd promontorie
> "Have I made shake, and by the spurs
> pluckt up."

There are also revealing title pages in other books, shewing a spear and an actor wearing a single spur only (see Plate 35, Page 153).

It will be of interest to shew another specially revealing title page, which for upwards of a hundred years remained unaltered as the title page to Vol. I. of Bacon's collected works, printed abroad in Latin. A different engraving, representing the same scene was also published in France. These engravings, however, were never reproduced or used in England, because the time for revelation had not yet come. Bacon is shewn seated (see Plate 33, Page 131). Compare his portrait with the engraving of the gentleman giving his scroll to the Spearman in the Gustavus Silenus frontispiece, Plate 27, Page 115, and Plate 28, Page 118. Bacon is pointing with his right hand in full light to his open book, while his left hand in deepest shadow is putting forward a figure holding in both its hands a closed and clasped book, which by the cross lines on its side (the accepted symbol of a mirror) shows that it represents the mirror up to Nature, *i.e.*, Shakespeare's plays. Specially note that Bacon puts forward with his LEFT hand the figure holding the book which is the mirror up to Nature. In the former part of this treatise the writer has proved that the figure that forms the frontispiece of the great folio of Shakespeare's plays, which is known as the Droeshout portrait of Wm. Shakespeare, is really composed of two LEFT arms and a mask. The reader will now be able to fully realise the revelation contained in Droeshout's masked figure with its two left arms when he examines it with the title page shown, Plate 33, Page 131.

Plate XXXIII.

FACSIMILE TITLE PAGE.

Plate XXXIII.

Facsimile Title Page.

Bacon is putting forward what we described as a "figure"; it is a "man" with false breasts to represent a woman (women were not permitted to act in Bacon's time), and the man is clothed in a goat skin. Tragedos was the Greek word for a goat skin, and Tragedies were so called because the actors were dressed in goat skins. This figure therefore represents the Tragic Muse. Here in the book called *De Augmentis Scientiarum*, which formed one part of the Great Instauration, is placed an engraving to show that another part of the Great Instauration known as Shakespeare's Plays was issued LEFT-HANDEDLY, that is, was issued under the name of a mean actor, the actor Shakespeare. This title page is very revealing, and should be taken in conjunction with the title page of the Cryptographic book which under the name of Gustavus Silenus, "*Homo lunæ*," the "Man in the Moon," was published in 1624 in order to form a key to certain cyphers in the 1623 Folio of Shakespeare's Plays.

These two title pages were prepared with consummate skill in order to reveal to the world, when the time was ripe, that

BACON IS SHAKESPEARE.

CHAPTER XII.

The "Householder of Stratford."

We have in Chapter II. printed Mr. George Hookham's list of the very few incidents recorded concerning Shakespeare's life, but, as we have already shewn, a great deal of the "authentic history" of the Stratford clown has in fact been revealed to us. Ben Jonson calls the Stratford man who had purchased a coat of arms "Sogliardo" (scum of the earth), says he was brother to Sordido, the miser (Shakspeare was a miser), describes him as an essential clown (that means that he was a rustic totally unable to read and write), shews that he speaks "i' th' straungest language," and calls Heralds "Harrots," and finally sums him up definitely as a "Swine without a head, without braine, wit, anything indeed, Ramping to Gentilitie." In order that there should be no mistake as to the man who is referred to, "Sogliardo's" motto is stated to be "Not without Mustard," Shakespeare's motto being "Not without right" (Non sanz droict). Ben Jonson's account of the real Stratford man is confirmed by Shakespeare's play of "As You Like it," where Touchstone, the courtier playing clown, says, "It is meat and drinke to me to see a clowne" (meaning an essential clown, an uneducated rustic); yet he salutes him as "gentle," shewing that the mean fellow possesses a coat of arms.

The Clown is born in the Forest of Ardennes (Shakespeare's mother's name was Arden). He is rich, but only so-so rich, that is rich for a clowne (New Place cost only £60). He says he is wise, and Touchstone mocks him with Bacon's words, "The Foole doth think he is wise, but the wise man knows himself to be a Fool." He says he has "a prettie wit" (pretty wit is the regular orthodox phrase as applied to Shakespeare). But when asked whether he is learned, he distinctly replies "No," which means that he says that he cannot read one line of print. A man who could read one line of print was at that period in the eye of the law "learned," and could not be hanged when convicted for the first time except for murder. If any persons be found to dispute the fact that the reply "No" to the question "Art thou learned?" meant in Queen Elizabeth's day "I cannot read one line of print" such persons must be totally unacquainted with Law literature.*

* About A.D. 1300 benefit of clergy was extended to all males who could read. In 1487 it was enacted that mere laymen should have the benefit only once and should be branded on the thumb to shew they had once had it. *Whimsies*, 1623, p. 69, tells us: "If a prisoner, by help of a compassionate prompter, hack out his neck verse (Psalm li. *v.* 1 in Latin) and be admitted to his clergy, the jailors have a cold iron in store if his purse be hot, but if not, a hot iron that his fist may *Fiz.*" Benefit of clergy was not totally abolished till 1827.

The play "As You Like it" confirms Ben Jonson's characterisation of Shakespeare being "an essential clowne." Next let us turn to Ratsei's *Ghost* (see p. 49), which, as Mr. Sidney Lee, in his "Life of William Shakespeare," p. 159, 1898 ed., confesses, refers to Shakespeare. Ratsei advises the young actor to copy Shakespeare, "and to feed upon all men, to let none feede upon thee" (meaning Shakespeare was a cruel usurer). As we shew, page 53, Grant White says: "The pursuit of an impoverished man for the sake of imprisoning him and depriving him both of the power of paying his debts and supporting himself and his family, is an incident in Shakespeare's life which it requires the utmost allowance and consideration for the practice of the time and country to enable us to contemplate with equanimity—satisfaction is impossible."

Ratsei continues, "Let thy hand be a stranger to thy pocket" [like the miser, Shakespeare], "thy hart slow to perform thy tongues promise" [like the lying rascal Shakespeare], and when thou feelest thy purse well lined, buy thee a place of lordship in the country" [as Shakespeare had bought New Place, Stratford] "that, growing weary of playing, thy mony may there bring thee to dignitie and reputation" [as Shakespeare obtained a coat of arms], "then thou needest care for no man, nor not for them that before made thee prowd with speaking their words upon the stage." This manifestly refers to two things, one that Shakespeare when he bought New Place, quitted London and ceased to act; the other that he continually tried to exact more and more "blackmail" from those to whom he had sold his name.

Now we begin at last to understand what we are told by Rowe, in his "Life of Shakespeare," published in 1709, that is, 93 years after Shakespeare's death in 1616, when all traces of the actual man had been of set purpose obliterated, because the time for revealing the real authorship of the plays had not yet come. Rowe, page x., tells us: "There is one Instance so singular in the Magnificence of this Patron of Shakespeare's, that if I had not been assur'd that the Story was handed down by Sir William D'Avenant, who was probably very well acquainted with his Affairs, I should not have ventured to have inserted, that my Lord Southampton, at one time, gave him a thousand Pounds, to enable him to go through with a Purchase which he heard he had a mind to."

This story has been hopelessly misunderstood, because people did not know that a large sum had to be paid to Shakespeare to obtain his consent to allow his name to be put to the plays, and that New Place had to be purchased for him, 1597 (the title deeds were not given to him for five or six years later), and that he had also to be sent away from London before "W Shakespeare's" name was attached to any play, the first play bearing that name being, as we have already pointed out, page 89, "Loues Labor's lost," with its very numerous revelations of authorship. Then, almost immediately, the world is informed that eleven other plays had been written by the same author, the list including the play of "Richard II."

The story of the production of the play of "Richard II." is very curious and extremely instructive. It was originally acted with the Parliament scene, where Richard II. is made to surrender, commencing in the Folio of 1623 with the words—

"Fetch hither Richard, that in common view
he may surrender,"

continuing with a description of his deposition extending over 167 lines to the words—

"That rise thus nimbly by a true king's fall."

This account of the deposition of a king reached Queen Elizabeth's ears; she was furiously angry and she exclaimed: "Seest thou not that I am Richard II."

A copy of the play without any author's name was printed in 1597, omitting the story of the deposition of Richard II.; this was followed by a second and probably a third reprint in 1597, with no important alterations, but still without any author's name. Then, after the actor had been sent away to Stratford, Shakespeare's name was put upon a fourth reprint, dated 1598.

The story of Richard II.'s deposition was not printed in the play till 1608,* five years after the death of Queen Elizabeth.

---

* In 1599 Sir John Hayward, LL.D., brought out "The Life and raigne of King Henrie IIII extending to the end of the first yeare of his raigne." This little book contains an account of the trial of Richard II., and was dedicated to the Earl of Essex in very encomiastic terms. It irritated Queen Elizabeth in the highest degree, and she clapped Hayward into prison and employed Sir Francis Bacon to search his book for treason. (Lowndes, Bohn, p. 1018). The story carefully read reveals the fact that it was really the play rather than the book which enraged Queen Elizabeth.

This history of the trouble arising out of the production of the play of "Richard II." explains why a name had to be found to be attached to the plays. Who would take the risk? An actor was never "hanged," he was often whipped, occasionally one lost his ears, but an actor of repute would probably have refused even a large bribe. There was, however, a grasping money-lending man, of little or no repute, that bore a name called Shaxpur, which might be twisted into Bacon's pen-name Shake-Speare, and that man was secured, but as long as he lived he was continually asking for more and more money. The grant of a coat of arms was probably part of the original bargain. At one time it seems to have been thought easier to grant arms to his father. This, however, was found impossible. But when in 1597 Bacon's friend Essex was Earl Marshal and chief of the Heralds' College, and Bacon's servant Camden (whom Bacon had assisted to prepare the "Annales"—see Spedding's "Bacon's Works," Vol. 6, p. 351, and Letters, Vol. 4, p. 211), was installed as Clarenceux, King-of-Arms, the grant of arms to Shakespeare was recognised, 1599. Shakespeare must have been provisionally secured soon after 1593, when the "Venus and Adonis" was signed with his name, because in the next year, 1594, "The Taming of a Shrew" was printed, in which the opening scene shews a drunken "Warwickshire" rustic [Shakspeare was a drunken Warwickshire rustic], who is dressed up as "My lord," for whom the play had been prepared. (In the writer's possession there is a very curious and absolutely unique masonic painting revealing "on the square" that the drunken tinker is Shakspeare and the Hostess, Bacon.)

The early date at which Shakspeare had been secured explains how in 1596 an application for a grant of arms seems to have been made (we say seems) for the date may possibly be a fraud like the rest of the lying document.

We have referred to Shakspeare as a drunken Warwickshire rustic who lived in the mean and dirty town of Stratford-on-Avon. There is a tradition that Shakespeare as a very young man was one of the Stratfordians selected to drink against "the Bidford topers," and with his defeated friends lay all night senseless under a crab tree, that was long known as Shakespeare's crab tree.

Shakespeare's description of the Stratford man as the drunken tinker in "The Taming of a Shrew" shews that the actor maintained his "drunken" character. This habit seems to have remained with him till the close of his life, for Halliwell-Phillipps says: "It is recorded that the party was a jovial one, and according to a somewhat late but apparently reliable tradition when the great dramatist [Shakespeare of Stratford] was returning to New Place in the evening, he had taken more wine than was conducive to pedestrian accuracy. Shortly or immediately afterwards he was seized by the lamentable fever which terminated fatally on Friday, April 23rd."

The story of his having to leave Stratford because

he got into very bad company and became one of a gang of deer-stealers, has also very early support.

We have already proved that Shakspeare could neither read nor write. We must also bear in mind that the Stratford man never had any reputation as an actor.

Rowe, p. vi., thus writes: "His Name is Printed, as the Custom was in those Times, amongst those of the other Players, before some old Plays,* but without any particular Account of what sort of Parts he us'd to play; and tho' I have inquir'd I could never meet with any further Account of him this way than that the top of his Performance was the Ghost in his own Hamlet." The humblest scene-shifter could play this character, as we shall shew later. What about being manager of a Theatre? Shakspeare never was manager of a Theatre. What about being master of a Shakespeare company of actors? There never existed a Shakespeare company of actors. What about ownership of a Theatre? Dr. Wallace, says in the *Times* of Oct. 2nd 1909, that at the time of his death Shakespeare owned one fourteenth of the Globe Theatre, and one-seventh of the Blackfriars Theatre. The profit of each of these was probably exceedingly small. The pleadings, put forth the present value at £300 each, but as a broad rule, pleadings always used to set forth at least ten times the actual facts. In the

* The appearance of Shakespeare's name in the list of Actors in Ben Jonson's plays and in the plays known as Shakespeare's was, of course, part of the plot to place Shakespeare's name in a prominent position while the pseudonym had to be preserved.

first case which the writer remembers witnessing in Court, the pleadings were 100 oxen, 100 cows, 100 calves, 100 sheep, and 100 pigs, the real matter in dispute being one cow and perhaps one calf. If we assume, therefore, that the total capital value of the holding of W. Shakespeare in both theatres taken together amounted to £60 in all, we shall probably, even then, considerably over-estimate their real worth. Now having disposed of the notion that Shakespeare was ever an important actor, was ever a manager of a Theatre, was ever the master of a company of actors, or was ever the owner of any Theatre, let us consider what Rowe means by the statement that the top of his performance was the Ghost in "Hamlet."

This grotesque and absurd fable has for two hundred years been accepted as an almost indisputable historical fact. Men of great intelligence in other matters seem when the life of Shakespeare of Stratford-on-Avon is concerned, quite prepared to refuse to exercise either judgment or common sense, and to swallow without question any amount of preposterous nonsense, even such as is contained in the above statement. The part of the Ghost in the play of "Hamlet" is one of the smallest and most insignificant possible, and can be easily played by the most ignorant and most inexperienced of actors. All that is required is a suit of armour with somebody inside it, to walk with his face concealed, silently and slowly a few times across the stage. Then on his final appearance he should say a few sentences (84 lines in the Folio,

1623), but these can be and occasionally are spoken by some invisible speaker in the same manner as the word "*Swear*," which is always growled out by someone concealed beneath the stage. No one knows, and no one cares, for no one sees who plays the part, which requires absolutely no histrionic ability. Sir Henry Irving, usually, I believe, put two men in armour upon the stage, in order to make the movements of the Ghost more mysterious. What then can be the meaning of the statement that the highest point to which the actor, Shakespeare, attained was to play the part of the *Ghost* in "Hamlet"? The rumour is so positive and so persistent that it cannot be disregarded or supposed to be merely a foolish jest or a senselessly false statement put forward for the purpose of deceiving the public. We are compelled, therefore, to conclude that there must be behind this fable some real meaning and some definite purpose, and we ask ourselves; What is the purpose of this puzzle? What can be its real meaning and intention? As usual, the Bacon key at once solves the riddle. The moment we realise that BACON is HAMLET, we perceive that the purpose of the rumour is to reveal to us the fact that the highest point to which the actor, Shakespeare, of Stratford-on-Avon, attained was to play the part of Ghost to Bacon, that is to act as his "PSEUDONYM," or in other words, the object of the story is to reveal to us the fact that

BACON IS SHAKESPEARE.

CHAPTER XIII.

Conclusion, with further evidences from title pages.

BACON had published eleven plays anonymously, when it became imperatively necessary for him to find some man who could be purchased to run the risk, which was by no means inconsiderable, of being supposed to be the author of these plays which included "Richard II."; the historical play which so excited the ire of Queen Elizabeth. Bacon, as we have already pointed out, succeeded in discovering a man who had little, if any, repute as an actor, but who bore a name which was called Shaxpur or Shackspere, which could be twisted into something that might be supposed to be the original of Bacon's pen name of Shake-Speare.

When in 1597 through the medium of powerful friends, by means of the bribe of a large sum of money, the gift of New Place, and the promise of a coat of arms, this man had been secured, he was at once sent away from London to the then remote village of Stratford-on-Avon, where scarcely a score of people could read, and none were likely to connect the name of their countryman, who they knew could neither read nor write and whom they called Shak or Shackspur, with "William Shakespeare" the author of plays the very names of which were absolutely unknown to any of them.

Bacon, when Shackspur had been finally secured in 1597, brought out in the following year 1598 "Loues Labor's lost" with the imprint "newly corrected and augmented by W. Shakespere," and immediately he also brought out under the name of Francis Meres "Wits Treasury," containing the statement that eleven other plays, including "Richard II.," were also by this same Shakespeare who had written the poems of "Venus and Adonis" and "Lucrece."

Francis Meres says: "As the soule of Euphorbus was thought to live in Pythagoras so the sweete wittie soule of Ovid lives in mellifluous and honytongued Shakespeare, witnes his 'Venus and Adonis,' his 'Lucrece,' his sugred Sonnets among his private friends."

The Sonnets were not printed, so far as is known, before 1609, and they as has been shown in Chapter 8 repeat the story of Bacon's authorship of the plays.

Bacon in 1598, as we have stated in previous pages, fully intended that at some future period posterity should do him justice.

Among his last recorded words are those in which he commends his name and fame to posterity, "after many years had past." Accordingly we find, as we should expect to find, that when he put Shakespeare's name to "Loues Labor's lost" (the first play to bear that name) Bacon took especial pains to secure that at some future date he should be recognised as the real author. Does he not clearly reveal this to us by the wonderful words with which the play of "Loues Labor's lost" opens?

"Let Fame, that all hunt after in their lyues,
Liue registred vpon our brazen Tombes,
And then grace vs, in the disgrace of death:
When spight of cormorant deuouring Time,
Thendeuour of this present breath may buy:
That honour which shall bate his sythes keene edge,
And make us heires of all eternitie."

Bacon intended that "Spight of cormorant devouring Time" . . . honour . . . . should make [him] heir of all eternitie.

Compare the whole of this grand opening passage of "Loues Labor's lost" with the lines ascribed to Milton in the 1632 edition of Shakespeare's plays when Bacon was [supposed to be] dead. No epitaph appeared in the 1623 edition, but in the 1632 edition appeared the following:—

"An Epitaph on the admirable Dramaticke Poet,
W. Shakespeare.

What neede my Shakespeare for his honour'd bones,
The labour of an Age in pilèd stones
Or that his hallow'd Reliques should be hid
Under a starrey-pointed Pyramid?

Deare sonne of Memory, great Heire of Fame,
What needst thou such dull witnesse of thy Name?
Thou in our wonder and astonishment
Hast built thy selfe a lasting Monument:
For whil'st, to th' shame of slow-endevouring Art
Thy easie numbers flow, and that each part,
Hath from the leaves of thy unvalued Booke,
Those Delphicke Lines with deepe impression tooke
Then thou our fancy of her selfe bereaving,
Dost make us Marble with too much conceiving,
And so Sepulcher'd, in such pompe dost lie
That Kings for such a Tombe would wish to die."

We have pointed out in Chapter 10 and in Chapter 11 how clearly in "Loues Labour's lost," on page 136 of the folio of 1623, Bacon reveals the fact that he is the Author of the Plays, and we have shewn how the title pages of certain books support this revelation, beginning with the title page of the first folio of 1623 with its striking revelation given to us in the supposititious portrait which really consists of "a mask supported on two left arms."

We may, however, perhaps here mention that instructions are specially given to all who can understand, in the little book which is said to be a continuation of Bacon's "Nova Atlantis," and to be by R. H., Esquire, [whom no one has hitherto succeeded in identifying].

On Plate 34, Page 149, we give a facsimile of its Title Page which describes the book and states that it was printed in 1660.

In this book a number of very extraordinary inventions are mentioned such as submarine boats to blow up ships and harbours, and telegraphy by means of magnetic needles, but the portion to which we now wish to allude is that which refers to a "solid kind of Heraldry." This will be found on pp. 23-4, and reads as follows:—

"We have a solid kind of Heraldry, not made specious with ostentative pydecoats and titular Atcheivements, which in Europe puzzel the tongue as well as memory to blazon, and any Fool may buy and wear for his money. Here in each province is a Register to record the memorable Acts, extraordinary qualities and worthy endowments of mind of the most eminent Patricians. Where for the Escutcheon of Pretence each noble person bears the Hieroglyphic of that vertue he is famous for. E.G. If eminent for Courage, the Lion; If for Innocence, the White Lamb; If for Chastity, a Turtle; If for Charity, the Sun in his full glory; If for Temperance, a slender Virgin, girt, having a bridle in her mouth; If for Justice, she holds a Sword in the right, and a Scales in the left hand; If for Prudence, she holds a Lamp; If for meek Simplicity, a Dove in her right hand; If for a discerning Judgment, an Eagle; If for Humility, she is in Sable, the head inclining and the knees bowing; If for Innocence, she holds a Lilie; If for Glory or Victory, a Garland of Baies; If for Wisdom, she holds a Salt; If he excels in Physic, an Urinal; If in Music, a Lute; If in Poetry, a Scrowle; If in Geometry, an Astrolabe; If in Arithmetic, a Table

New Atlantis.

Begun by the

LORD VERULAM,

VISCOUNT St. *Albans*:

AND

Continued by R. H. Esquire.

Wherein is set forth

A PLATFORM

OF

MONARCHICAL GOVERNMENT.

WITH

A Pleasant intermixture of divers rare Inventions, and wholsom Customs, fit to be introduced into all KINGDOMS, STATES, and COMMON-WEALTHS.

——*Nunquam Libertas gratior extat*
Quam sub Rege pio.

LONDON,
Printed for *John Crooke* at the Signe of the Ship in St. *Pauls* Church-yard, *1660*.

Plate XXXIV.

FACSIMILE TITLE PAGE.

Plate XXXIV.

Facsimile of Title Page of New Atlantis,
continued by R. H., Esquire, 1660.

of Cyphers; If in Grammar, an Alphabetical Table; If in Mathematics, a Book; If in Dialectica she holds a Serpent in either hand; and so of the rest; the Pretence being ever paralel to his particular Excellency. And this is sent him cut in brass, and in colours, as he best phansies for the Field; only the Hieroglyphic is alwayes proper."

These references to a solid kind of Heraldry refer to the title pages and frontispieces of books which may be characterised broadly as Baconian books, and examples of every one of them can be found in books extending from the Elizabethan period almost up to the present date.

We place Plate 35, Page 153, before the reader, which is a photo enlargement of the title page of Bacon's "History of Henry VII.," printed in Holland, 1642, the first Latin edition (in 12mo).

Here is seen the Virgin holding the Salt, shewing the Wisdom of the Author. In her right hand, which holds the Salt, she holds also two other objects which seem difficult to describe. They represent "a bridle without a bit," in order to tell us the purpose of the Plate is to unmuzzle Bacon, and to reveal to us his authorship of the plays known as Shakespeare's.

But in order to prove that the objects represent a bridle without a bit, we must refer to two emblem books of very different dates and authorship.

First we refer our readers to Plate 36, Page 156, which is a photo enlargement of the figure of Nemesis in the first (February 1531) edition of Alciati's Emblems.

The picture shews us a hideous figure holding in her left hand a bridle with a tremendous bit to destroy false reputations, *improba verba.*

We next put before our readers the photo reproduction of the figure of Nemesis, which will be found on page 484, of Baudoin's Emblems, 1638. Baudoin had previously brought out in French a translation of Bacon's "Essays," which was published at Paris in 1621. In the preface to his book of Emblems he tells us that he was induced to undertake the task by BACON (printed in capital letters), and by Alciat (printed in ordinary type). In this book of Emblems, Baudoin, on page 484, placed his figure of Nemesis opposite to Bacon's name. If the reader carefully examines Plate 37 he will perceive that it is no longer a grinning hideous figure, but is a figure of FAME, and carries a bridle in which there is found to be no sign of any kind of bit, because the purpose of the Emblem is to shew that Nemesis will unmuzzle and glorify Bacon.

In order to make the meaning of Baudoin's Emblem still more emphatically explicit a special Rosicrucian Edition of the same date, 1638, was printed, in which Baudoin's Nemesis is printed "upside down"; we do not mean bound upside down, but printed upside down, for there is the printing of the previous page at the back of the engraving. We have already alluded on page 113 to the frequent practice of the upside down printing of ornaments and engravings when a revelation concerning Bacon's connection with Shakespeare is afforded to us.

Plate XXXV.

FACSIMILE TITLE PAGE.

Plate XXXV.

FACSIMILE TITLE PAGE OF BACON'S HENRY VII., 1642.

Plate XXXVI.

"Nemesis," from Alciati's Emblems, 1531.

Plate XXXVI.

'Nemesis," from Alciati's Emblems, 1531.

Plate XXXVII.

PAGE 484 FROM BAUDOIN'S EMBLEMS, 1638.

Plate XXXVII.

Page 484 from Baudoin's Emblems, 1638.

The writer possesses an ordinary copy of Baudoin's Emblems, 1638, and also a copy of the edition with the Nemesis printed upside down which appears opposite Bacon's name. The copy so specially printed is bound with Rosicrucian emblems outside.

The reader, by comparing Baudoin's Nemesis, Plate 37, and the Title Page of Henry VII., Plate 35, will at once perceive that the objects in the right hand of the Virgin holding the salt box are correctly described as representing a "bridle without a bit," and he will know that a revelation concerning Bacon and Shakespeare is going to be given to him. Now we will tell him the whole story. On the right of the picture, Plate 35 (the reader's left) we see a knight in full armour, and also a philosopher who is, as the roses on his shoes tell us, a Rosicrucian philosopher. On the left on a lower level is the same philosopher, evidently Bacon, but without the roses on his shoes. He is holding the shaft of a spear with which he seems to stop the wheel. By his side stands what appears to be a Knight or Esquire, but the man's sword is girt on the wrong side, he wears a lace collar and lace trimming to his breeches, and he wears actor's boots (see Plate 28, Page 118, and Plate 132, Page 127).

We are therefore forced to conclude that he is an Actor. And, lo, he wears but ONE SPUR. He is therefore a Shake-spur Actor (on Plate 27, Page 115, is shewn a Shake-spur on horseback). This same Actor is also shaking the spear which is held by the philosopher. He is therefore also a Shake-spear Actor.

And now we can read the symbols on the wheel which is over his head: the "mirror up to nature," "the rod for the back of fools," the "basin to hold your guilty blood ("Titus Andronicus," v. 2), and "the fool's bawble." On the other side of the spear: the spade the symbol of the workman, the cap the symbol of the gentleman, the crown the symbol of the peer, the royal crown, and lastly the Imperial crown. Bacon says Henry VII. wore an Imperial crown. Quite easily now we can read the whole story.

The "History of Henry VII.," though in this picture displayed on a stage curtain, is set forth by Bacon in prose while the rest of the Histories of England are given to the world by Bacon by means of his pseudonym the Shake-spear Actor at the Globe to which that figure is pointing.

Plain as the plate appears to the instructed eye it seems hitherto to have failed to reveal to the *un*instructed its clear meaning that

BACON IS SHAKE-SPEARE.

CHAPTER XIV.

Postscriptum.

Most fortunately before going to press we were able to see at the Record Office, Chancery Lane, London, the revealing documents recently discovered by Dr. Wallace and described by him in an article published in the March number of *Harper's Monthly Magazine*, under the title of "New Shakespeare Discoveries." The documents found by Dr. Wallace are extremely valuable and important. They tell us a few real facts about the Householder of Stratford-upon-Avon, and they effectually once and for all dispose of the idea that the Stratford man was the Poet and Dramatist,—the greatest genius of all the ages.

In the first place they prove beyond the possibility of cavil or question that "Shakespeare, of Stratford-upon-Avon, Gentleman," was totally unable to write even so much as any portion of his own name. It is true that the Answers to the Interrogatories which are given by "William Shakespeare, of Stratford-upon-Avon, Gentleman," are marked at the bottom "Wilm Shaxp^r^," but this is written by the lawyer or law clerk, in fact "dashed in" by the ready pen of an extremely rapid writer. A full size photographic facsimile of this "so-called" signature, with a portion of the document above it, is given in Plate 38, Page 164, and on the opposite page, in Plate 39, is shewn also in full size facsimile the real signature of Daniell Nicholas with a portion of the document, which he signed, above it.

In order that the reader may be able more easily to read the law writing we give on page 167, in modern type, the portion of the document photographed above the name Wilm Shaxp[r], and on the same page a modern type transcript of the document above the signature of Daniell Nicholas.

Any expert in handwriting will at once perceive that "Wilm Shaxp[r]" is written by the same hand that wrote the lower portion of Shakespeare's Answers to Interrogatories, and by the same hand that wrote the other set of Answers to Interrogatories which are signed very neatly by "Daniell Nicholas."

The words "Daughter Marye" occur in the portion photographed of both documents, and are evidently written by the same law writer, and can be seen in Plate 38, Page 164, just above the "Wilm Shaxp[r]," and in Plate 39, Page 165, upon the fifth line from the top. The name of "Shakespeare" also occurs several times in the "Answers to Interrogatories." One instance occurs in Plate 39, Page 165, eight lines above the name of Daniell Nicholas, and if the reader compares it with the "Wilm Shaxp[r]" on Plate 38, Page 164, it will be at once seen that both writings are by the same hand.

Plate XXXVIII.

Full Size Facsimile of part of "Shakespeare's Answers to Interrogatories," discovered by Dr. Wallace in the British Record Office.

Plate XXXVIII.

Full Size Facsimile of part of "Shakespeare's Answers to Interrogatories," discovered by Dr. Wallace in the British Record Office.

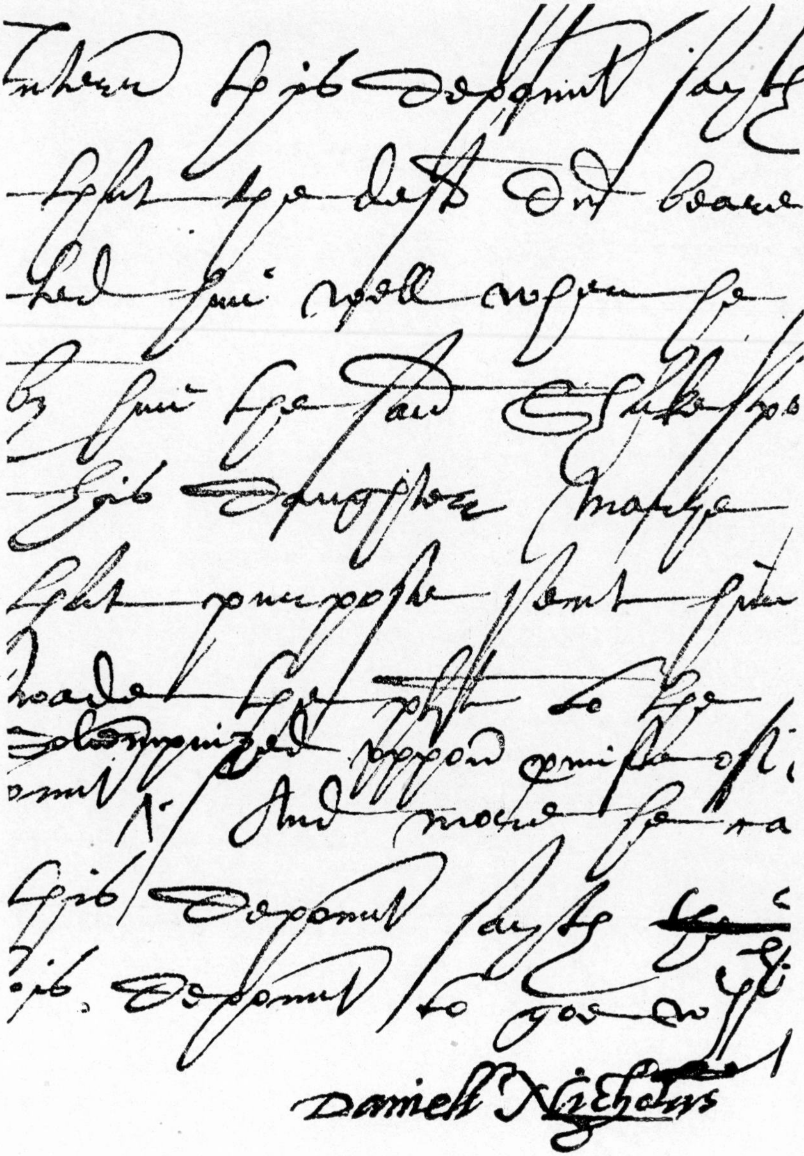

Plate XXXIX.

Full Size Facsimile of part of Daniell Nicholas' "Answers to Interrogatories," discovered by Dr. Wallace in the British Record Office.

Plate XXXIX.

Full Size Facsimile of part of Daniell Nicholas' "Answers to Interrogatories," discovered by Dr. Wallace in the British Record Office.

portion
What c'tayne ^ he

. . . . . .

. plt twoe hundered pounds
decease. But sayth that
his house. And they had amo
about their marriadge w^ch
nized. And more he can
ponnt saythe he can saye
of the same Interro for
cessaries of houshould stuffe
his daughter Marye

WILM SHAXPR

Type Facsimile of Plate XXXVIII.

Interr this depnnt sayth
that the deft did beare
ted him well when he
by him the said Shakespeare
his daughter Marye
that purpose sent him
swade the plt to the
solempnised uppon pmise of
nnt. And more he can
this deponnt sayth
is deponnt to goe w^th

DANIELL NICHOLAS.

Type Facsimile of Plate XXXIX.

Answers to Interrogatories are required to be signed by the deponents. In the case of "Johane Johnsone," who could not write her name, the depositions are signed with a very neat cross which was her mark. In the case of "William Shakespeare, of Stratford-upon-Avon, Gentleman," who was also unable to write his name, they are signed with a dot which might quite easily be mistaken for an accidental blot. Our readers will see this mark, which is not a blot but a purposely made mark, just under "Wilm Shaxp[r]."

Dr. Wallace reads the "so-called" signature as Willm Shaks, but the Christian name is written quite clearly Wilm. And we should have supposed that any one possessing even the smallest acquaintance with the law writing of the period must have known that the scroll which looks like a flourish at the end of the surname is not and cannot be an "s," but is most certainly without any possibility of question a "p," and that the dash through the "p" is the usual and accepted abbreviation for words ending in "per," or "peare," etc.* Then how ought we, nay how are

* Facsimiles of law clerks' writing of the name "John Shakespeare," are given in Plate 40, Page 169. They are taken from Halliwell-Phillipps' "Outlines of the Life of Shakespeare," 1889, vol. 2, pp. 233 and 236. In the first two examples the name is written "Shakes," followed by an exactly similar scroll and dash to complete the name. In Saunders' "Ancient Handwriting," 1909, page 24, we are shown that such a "scroll and dash" represents "per" "par," and "por"; and in Wright's "Court Handwriting restored" we find that in the most perfectly formed script a "p" with a dash through the lower part similarly represented "per," "par," and "por," this is repeated in Thoyts' "How to decipher and study old documents," and the same information is given in numerous other works. There is therefore no possible excuse for Dr. Wallace's blundering.

we, compelled to read the so-called signature? The capital S is quite clear, so also is the "h," then the next mass of strokes all go to make up simply the letter "a." Then we come to the blotted letter,

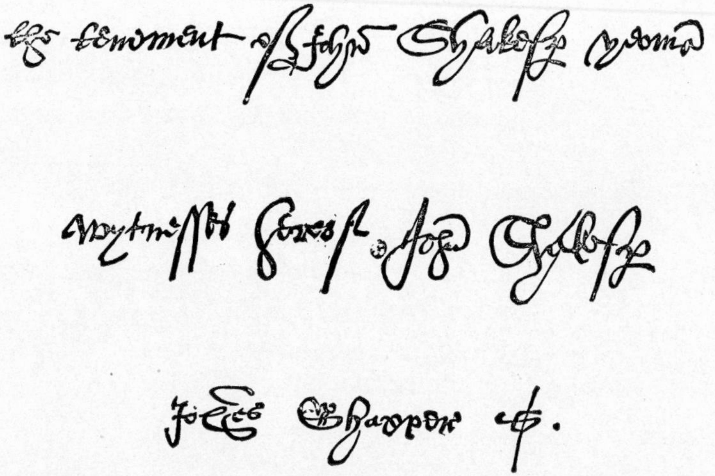

Plate XL.

FACSIMILES OF LAW CLERKS' WRITING OF THE NAME "SHAKESPEARE," FROM HALLIWELL-PHILLIPPS' "OUTLINES OF THE LIFE OF SHAKESPEARE," VOL. 2, 1889.

this is not and cannot be "kes" or "ks" because in the law writing of the period every letter "s" (excepting "s" at the end of a word) was written as a very long letter. This may readily be seen in the word Shakespeare which occurs in Plate 39 on the eighth line above the signature of Daniell Nicholas.

What then is this blotted letter if it is not kes or ks? The answer is quite plain, it is an "X," and a careful examination under a very strong magnifying glass will satisfy the student that it is without possibility of question correctly described as an "X."* Yes, the law clerk marked the Stratford Gentleman's "Answers to Interrogatories" with the name "Wilm Shaxp^{r}." Does there exist a Stratfordian who will contend that William Shakespeare, of Stratford-upon-Avon, Gentleman, if he had been able to write any portion of his name would have marked his depositions Wilm Shaxp^{r}? Does there exist any man who will venture to contend that the great Dramatist, the author of the Immortal plays, would or could have so signed his name? We trow not; indeed, such an abbreviation would be impossible in a legal document in a Court of Law where depositions are required to be signed in full.

With reference to the other so-called Shakespeare's signatures we must refer the reader to our Chapter III. which was penned before these "New Shakespeare Discoveries" were announced. And it is perhaps desirable to say that the dot in the "W" which appears in two of those "so-called" signatures of Shakespeare, and also in the one just discovered, is part of the regular method of writing a "W" in the law writing of the period. In the Purchase Deed of the property in Blackfriars, of March 10th 1612-13, mentioned on page 38, there are

* A facsimile example of the way in which the law clerk wrote "Shaxper" is shewn in the third line of Plate 40, Page 169, where it will be seen that the writer uses a similar "X."

in the first six lines of the Deed seven "W's," in each of which appears a dot. And in the Mortgage Deed of March 11th 1612-13, there are seven "W's" in the first five lines, in each of which appears a similar dot. The above-mentioned two Deeds are in the handwriting of different law clerks.

It may not be out of place here again to call our readers' attention to the fact that law documents are required to be signed "in full," and that if the very rapid and ready writer who wrote "Wilm Shaxp^{r}" were indeed the Gentleman of Stratford it would have been quite easy for such a good penman to have written his name in full; this the law writer has not done because he did not desire to forge a signature to the document, but desired only to indicate by an abbreviation that the dot or spot below was the mark of William Shakespeare of Stratford-upon-Avon.

Thus the question, whether William Shakespeare, of Stratford-upon-Avon, Gentleman, could or could not write his name is for ever settled in the negative, and there is no doubt, there can be no doubt, upon this matter.

Dr. Wallace declares "I have had no theory to defend and no hypothesis to propose." But as a matter of fact his whole article falsely assumes that "William Shakespeare, of Stratford-upon-Avon, Gentleman," who is referred to in the documents, is no other than the great Dramatist who wrote the Immortal plays. And the writer can only express his unbounded wonder and astonishment that even so ardent a

Stratfordian as Dr. Wallace, after studying the various documents which he discovered, should have ventured to say:

> "Shakespeare was the third witness examined. Although, forsooth, the matter of his statements is of no high literary quality and the manner is lacking in imagination and style, as the Rev. Joseph Green in 1747 complained of the will, we feel none the less as we hear him talk that we have for the first time met Shakespeare in the flesh and that the acquaintance is good."

As a matter of fact none of the words of any of the deponents are their own words, but they are the words of the lawyers who drew the Answers to the Interrogatories. The present writer, when a pupil in the chambers of a distinguished lawyer who afterwards became a Lord Justice, saw any number of Interrogatories and Answers to Interrogatories, and even assisted in their preparation. The last thing that any one of the pupils thought of, was in what manner the client would desire to express his own views. They drew the most plausible Answers they could imagine, taking care that their words were sufficiently near to the actual facts for the client to be able to swear to them.

The so-called signature "Wilm Shaxp^{r}," is written by the lawyer or law clerk who wrote the lower part of Shakespeare's depositions, and this same clerk also wrote the depositions above the name of another witness who really *signs* his own name, viz., "Daniell Nicholas." The only mark William Shakespeare put to the document was the blot above which the abbreviated name "Wilm Shaxp[r]" was written by the lawyer or law clerk.

The documents shew that Shakespeare of Stratford occasionally "lay" in the house in Silver Street, and Ben Jonson's words in "The Staple of News" (Third Intermeane; Act iii.), to which Dr. Wallace refers viz., that "Siluer-Streete" was "a good seat for a Vsurer" are very informing, because as we have before pointed out the Stratford man was a cruel usurer.

Dr. Wallace's contention that Mountjoy, the wig-maker, of the corner house in Silver Street where Shakespeare, of Stratford-upon-Avon, Gentleman, occasionally slept, was the original of the name of the Herald in Henry V.* really surpasses, in want of knowledge of History, anything that the writer has ever previously encountered, and he is afraid that it really is a measure of the value of Dr. Wallace's other inferences connecting the illiterate Stratford Rustic with the great Dramatist who "took all knowledge for his province."

Dr. Wallace's "New Shakespeare Discoveries" are really extremely valuable and informing, and very greatly assist the statements which the writer has made in the previous chapters, viz., that the Stratford Householder was a mean Rustic who was totally

* Holinshed's Chronicles (1557) state that "Montioy, king-at-arms, was sent to the King of England to defie him as the enemie of France, and to tell him that he should shortlie have battell." Moreover, "Montioy" is not the personal name, but the official title of a Herald of France, just as "Norroy" is not a personal name, but the official title of one of the three chief Heralds of the College of Arms of England.

unable to read or to write, and was not even an actor of repute, but was a mere hanger-on at the Theatre. Indeed, the more these important documents are examined the clearer it will be perceived that, as Dr. Wallace points out, they shew us that the real William Shakespeare, of Stratford-upon-Avon, gentleman, was not the "Aristocrat," whom Tolstoi declares the author of the plays to have been, but was in fact a man who resided [occasionally when he happened to revisit London] "in a hardworking family," a man who was familiar with hairdressers and their apprentices, a man who mixed as an equal among tradesmen in a humble position of life, who referred to him as "One Shakespeare." These documents prove that "One Shakespeare" was not and could not have been the "poet and dramatist." In a word these documents strongly confirm the fact that

BACON IS SHAKESPEARE.

Plate XLI.

Facsimile of the Dedication of Powell's "Attourney's Academy," 1630.

TO
TRVE NOBILITY,
AND TRYDE LEARNING,

BEHOLDEN

To no Mountaine for Eminence, nor Supportment for Height, FRANCIS, Lord *Verulam*, and Viſcount St, *Albanes.*

O Giue me leaue to pull the Curtaine by,
That clouds thy Worth in ſuch obſcurity,
Good *Seneca*, ſtay but a while thy bleeding,
T'accept what I receiued at thy Reading:
Here I preſent it in a ſolemne ſtrayne,
And thus I pluckt the Curtayne backe againe.

The ſame

THOMAS POWELL.

Plate XLI.

FACSIMILE OF THE DEDICATION OF POWELL'S "ATTOURNEY'S ACADEMY," 1630.

CHAPTER XV.

Appendix.

THE facsimile shewn in Plate 41, Page 176, is from "The Attourney's Academy," 1630. The reader will perceive that the ornamental heading is printed upside down. In the ordinary copies it is not so printed, but only in special copies such as that possessed by the writer; the object of the upside-down printing being, as we have already pointed out in previous pages, to reveal, to those deemed worthy of receiving it, some secret concerning Bacon.

In the present work, while we have used our utmost endeavour to place in the vacant frame, the true portrait of him who was the wonder and mystery of his own age and indeed of all ages, we have never failed to remember the instructions given to us in "King Lear":—

> "Have more than thou showest,
> Speak less than thou knowest."

Our object has been to supply exact and positive information and to confirm it by proofs so accurate and so certain as to compel belief and render any effective criticism an impossibility.

N

It may however not be without advantage to those who are becoming convinced against their will, if we place before them a few of the utterances of men of the greatest distinction who, without being furnished with the information which we have been able to afford to our readers, were possessed of sufficient intelligence and common sense to perceive the truth respecting the real authorship of the Plays.

LORD PALMERSTON, b. 1784, d. 1865.

Viscount Palmerston, the great British statesman, used to say that he rejoiced to have lived to see three things—the re-integration of Italy, the unveiling of the mystery of China and Japan, and the explosion of the Shakespearian illusions.—*From the Diary of the Right Hon. Mount-Stewart E. Grant.*

LORD HOUGHTON, b. 1809, d. 1885.

Lord Houghton (better known as a statesman under the name of Richard Monckton Milnes) reported the words of Lord Palmerston, and he also told Dr. Appleton Morgan that he himself no longer considered Shakespeare, the actor, as the author of the Plays.

SAMUEL TAYLOR COLERIDGE, b. 1772, d. 1834.

Samuel Taylor Coleridge, the eminent British critic and poet, although he assumed that Shakespeare was the author of the Plays, rejected the facts of his life and character, and says: "Ask your own hearts, ask your own common sense, to conceive the possibility of the author of the Plays being the anomalous, the wild, the irregular genius of our daily criticism.

What! are we to have miracles in sport? Does God choose idiots by whom to convey divine truths to man?"

JOHN BRIGHT, b. 1811, d. 1889.

John Bright, the eminent British statesman, declared: "Any man that believes that William Shakespeare of Stratford wrote Hamlet or Lear is a fool." In its issue of March 27th 1889, the *Rochdale Observer* reported John Bright as scornfully angry with deluded people who believe that Shakespeare wrote Othello.

RALPH WALDO EMERSON, b. 1803, d. 1882.

Ralph Waldo Emerson, the great American philosopher and poet, says: "As long as the question is of talent and mental power, the world of men has not his equal to show. . . . . . The Egyptian verdict of the Shakespeare Societies comes to mind that he was a jovial actor and manager. I cannot marry this fact to his verse."—*Emerson's Works. London, 1883. Vol. 4, p. 420.*

JOHN GREENLEAF WHITTIER, b. 1807, d. 1892.

John Greenleaf Whittier, the American poet, declared: "Whether Bacon wrote the wonderful plays or not, I am quite sure the man Shakspere neither did nor could."

DR. W. H. FURNESS, b. 1802, d. 1891.

Dr. W. H. Furness, the eminent American scholar, who was the father of the Editor of the Variorum

Edition of Shakespeare's Works, wrote to Nathaniel Holmes in a letter dated Oct. 29th 1866: "I am one of the many who have never been able to bring the life of William Shakespeare and the plays of Shakespeare within planetary space of each other. Are there any two things in the world more incongruous? Had the plays come down to us anonymously, had the labor of discovering the author been imposed upon after generations, I think we could have found no one of that day but F. Bacon to whom to assign the crown. In this case it would have been resting now on his head by almost common consent."

MARK TWAIN, b. 1835, d. 1910.

Samuel Langhorne Clemens, who wrote under the pseudonym of Mark Twain, was,—it is universally admitted,—one of the wisest of men. Last year (1909) he published a little book with the title, "Is Shakespeare dead?" In this he treats with scathing scorn those who can persuade themselves that the immortal plays were written by the Stratford clown. He writes, pp. 142-3: "You can trace the life histories of the whole of them [the world's celebrities] save one—far and away the most colossal prodigy of the entire accumulation—Shakespeare. About him you can find out *nothing*. Nothing of even the slightest importance. Nothing worth the trouble of stowing away in your memory. Nothing that even remotely indicates that he was ever anything more than a distinctly commonplace person—a manager,* an actor of inferior grade, a

* He never was a manager.

small trader in a small village that did not regard him as a person of any consequence, and had forgotten him before he was fairly cold in his grave. We can go to the records and find out the life-history of every renowned *race-horse* of modern times—but not Shakespeare's! There are many reasons why, and they have been furnished in cartloads (of guess and conjecture) by those troglodytes; but there is one that is worth all the rest of the reasons put together, and is abundantly sufficient all by itself—*he hadn't any history to record.* There is no way of getting around that deadly fact. And no sane way has yet been discovered of getting round its formidable significance. Its quite plain significance—to any but those thugs (I do not use the term unkindly) is, that Shakespeare had no prominence while he lived, and none until he had been dead two or three generations. The Plays enjoyed high fame from the beginning."

PRINCE BISMARCK, b. 1815, d. 1898.

We are told in Sydney Whitman's "Personal Reminiscences of Prince Bismarck," pp. 135-6, that in 1892, Prince Bismarck said, "He could not understand how it were possible that a man, however gifted with the intuitions of genius, could have written what was attributed to Shakespeare unless he had been in touch with the great affairs of state, behind the scenes of political life, and also intimate with all the social courtesies and refinements of thought which in Shakspeare's time were only to be met with in the highest circles.

"It also seemed to Prince Bismarck incredible that the man who had written the greatest dramas in the world's literature could of his own free will, whilst still in the prime of life, have retired to such a place as Stratford-on-Avon and lived there for years, cut off from intellectual society, and out of touch with the world."

The foregoing list of men of the very greatest ability and intelligence who were able clearly to perceive the absurdity of continuing to accept the commonly received belief that the Mighty Author of the immortal Plays was none other than the mean rustic of Stratford, might be extended indefinitely, but the names that we have mentioned are amply sufficient to prove to the reader that he will be in excellent company when he himself realises the truth that

BACON IS SHAKESPEARE.

A NEUER WRITER, TO AN EUER READER . NEWES.

ETERNALL reader, you haue heere a new play, neuer stal'd with the Stage, neuer clapper-clawd with the palmes of the vulger, and yet passing full of the palme comicall; for it is a birth of your braine, that neuer under-tooke any thing commicall, vainely: And were but the vaine names of commedies changde for the titles of Commodities, or of Playes for Pleas; you should see all those grand censors, that now stile them such vanities, flock to them for the maine grace of their grauities: especially this authors Commedies, that are so fram'd to the life, that they serve for the most common Commentaries, of all the actions of our liues shewing such a dexteritie, and power of witte, that the most displeased with Playes are pleasd with his Commedies. . . . .

And beleeue this, that when hee is gone, and his Commedies out of sale, you will scramble for them, and set up a new English Inquisition. Take this for a warning, and at the perrill of your pleasures losse, and Judgements, refuse not, nor like this the lesse, for not being sullied, with the smoaky breath of the multitude.

From the Introduction of "The Famous Historie of Troylus and Cresseid, by William Shakespeare," 1609. This play as the above Introduction says was never acted.

PROMUS

OF

FOURMES AND ELEGANCYES

BY

FRANCIS BACON.

PREFACE TO PROMUS.

To these Essays I have attached a carefully collated reprint of Francis Bacon's "Promus of Formularies and Elegancies," a work which is to be found in Manuscript at the British Museum in the Harleian Collection (No. 7,017.)

The folios at present known are numbered from 83 to 132, and are supposed to have been written about A.D. 1594-6, because folio 85 is dated December 5th 1594, and folio 114, January 27 1595.

The pagination of the MS. is modern, and was inserted for reference purposes when the Promus was bound up in one volume together with certain other miscellaneous manuscripts which are numbered from 1 to 82, and from 133 onwards.

A facsimile of a portion of a leaf of the Promus MS., folio 85, is given on pages 190-91, in order to illustrate Bacon's handwriting, and also to shew his method of marking the entries. It will be perceived that some entries have lines / / / / drawn across the writing, while upon others marks similar to the capital letters T, F, and A are placed at the end of the lines. But as the Promus is here printed page for page as in the manuscript, I am not raising the question of the signification of these marks, excepting only to say they indicate that Bacon made considerable use of these memoranda.

"Promus" means larder or storehouse, and these "Fourmes, Formularies and Elegancyes" appear to have been intended as a storehouse of words and phrases to be employed in the production of subsequent literary works.

Mrs. Pott was the first to print the "Promus," which, with translations and references, she published in 1883. In her great work, which really may be described as monumental, Mrs. Pott points out, by means of some thousands of quotations, how great a use appears to have been made of the "Promus" notes, both in the acknowledged works of Bacon and in the plays which are known as Shakespeare's.

Mrs. Pott's reading of the manuscript was extremely good, considering the great difficulty experienced in deciphering the writing. But I thought it advisable when preparing a reprint to secure the services of the late Mr. F. B. Bickley, of the British Museum, to carefully revise the whole of Bacon's "Promus." This task he completed and I received twenty-four proofs, which I caused to be bound with a title page in 1898. There were no other copies, the whole of the type having unfortunately been broken up. The proof has again been carefully collated with the original manuscript and corrected by Mr. F. A. Herbert, of the British Museum, and I have now reprinted it here, as I am satisfied that the more Bacon's Promus—the Storehouse—is examined, the more it will be recognised how large a portion of the material collected therein has been made use of in the Immortal Plays, and I therefore now issue the Promus with the present essay as an additional proof of the identity of Bacon and Shakespeare.

EDWIN DURNING-LAWRENCE.

Dec 5. 1594.

Orenus.

~~Ex nequissima vita~~ indies meliorem fieri

The grace of God is worth a faire.

Mors in olla. tu

No wise ~~speech~~ though easily had would bee.

Notwithstanding his dialogues (whose their greatest life be his speach by way of question.)

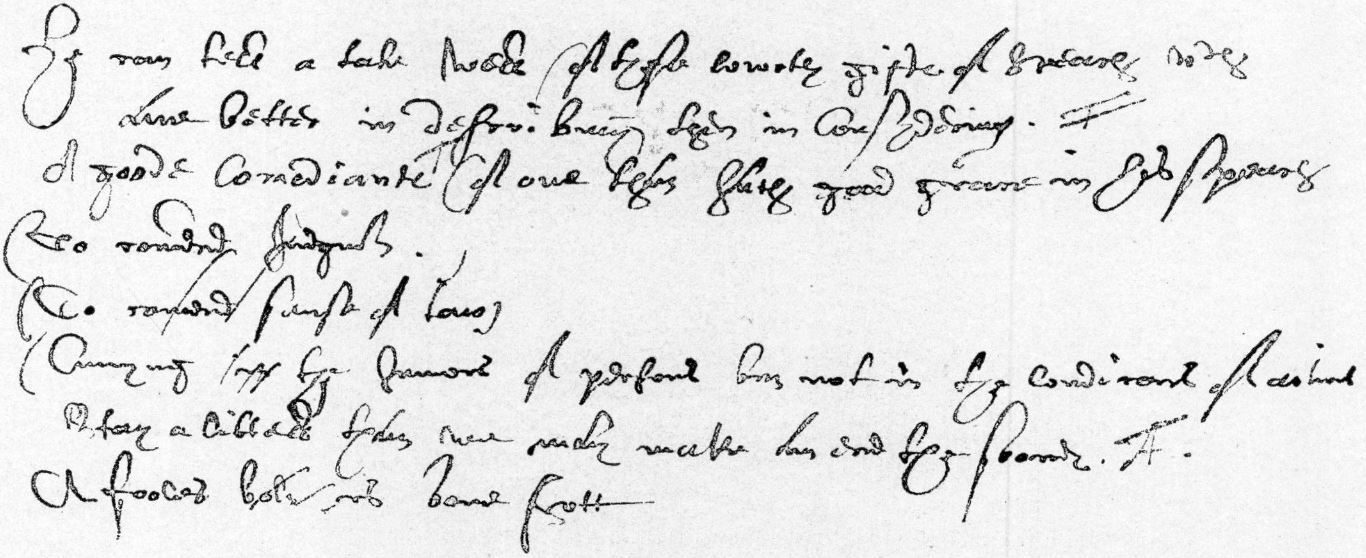

Plate XLII.

Facsimile of portion of Folio 85 of the Original MS. of Bacon's "Promus." See page 199.

Plate XLIII.

Portrait of Francis Bacon, from a Painting by Van Somer, formerly in the Collection of the Duke of Fife.

Promus of Formularies.

Folio 83, front.

Ingenuous honesty and yet with opposition and strength.

Corni contra croci good means against badd, hornes to crosses.

In circuitu ambulant impij; honest by antiperistasis.

Siluj a bonis et dolor meus renouatus est.

Credidj propter quod locutus sum.

Memoria justi cum laudibus at impiorum nomen putrescet

Justitiamque omnes cupida de mente fugarunt.

Non recipit stultus verba prudentiæ nisi ea dixeris quæ uersantur in corde ejus

Veritatem eme et noli vendere

Qui festinat ditari non erat insons

Nolite dare sanctum canibus.

Qui potest capere capiat

Quoniam Moses ad duritiam cordis uestri permisit uobis

Obedire oportet deo magis quam hominibus.

Et vniuscujusque opus quale sit probabit ignis

Non enim possumus aliquid aduersus ueritatem sed pro ueritate.

Folio 83, front—continued.

For which of ye good woorkes doe yow stone me

Quorundam hominum peccata præcedunt ad judicium quorundam sequuntur

Bonum certamen certauj

Sat patriæ priamoque datum.

Ilicet obruimur numero.

Atque animis illabere nostris

Hoc prætexit nomine culpam.

Procul ô procul este prophani

Magnanimj heroes nati melioribus annis

Folio 83, back.

Ille mihi ante alios fortunatusque laborum
Egregiusque animi qui ne quid tale videret
Procubuit moriens et humum semel ore momordit
Fors et uirtus miscentur in vnum.
Non ego naturâ nec sum tam callidus vsu.
æuo rarissima nostro simplicitas
Viderit vtilitas ego cepta fideliter edam.
Prosperum et fœlix scelus, virtus vocatur
Tibi res antiquæ laudis et artis
Inuidiam placare paras uirtute relicta.
Iliacos intra muros peccatur et extra
Homo sum humanj a me nil alienum puto.
The grace of God is woorth a fayre
Black will take no other hue
Vnum augurium optimum tueri patrià.
Exigua res est ipsa justitia
Dat veniam coruis uexat censura columbas.
Homo hominj deus
Semper virgines furiæ; Cowrting a furye
Di danarj di senno et di fede
Cè nè manco che tu credj
Chi semina spine non vada discalzo
Mas vale a quien Dios ayuda que a quien mucho madruga.
Quien nesciamente pecca nesciamente ua al infierno
Quien ruyn es en su uilla
Ruyn es en Seuilla
De los leales se hinchen los huespitales

Folio 84, front.

We may doe much yll or we doe much woorse
Vultu læditur sæpe pietas.
Difficilia quæ pulchra
Conscientia mille testes.
Summum Jus summa injuria
Nequicquam patrias tentasti lubricus artes.
Et monitj meliora sequamur
Nusquam tuta fides
Discite Justitiam moniti et non temnere diuos
Quisque suos patimur manes.
Extinctus amabitur idem.
Optimus ille animi vindex lædentium pectus
Vincula qui rupit dedoluitque semel.
Virtue like a rych geme best plaine sett
Quibus bonitas a genere penitus insita est
ij iam non mali esse nolunt sed nesciunt
Oeconomicæ rationes publicas peruertunt.
Divitiæ Impedimenta virtutis; The bagage of vertue
Habet et mors aram.
Nemo virtuti invidiam reconciliauerit præter mort . . .
Turpe proco ancillam sollicitare Est autem virtutis ancilla laus.
Si suum cuique tribuendum est certè et venia humanitati
Qui dissimulat liber non est
Leue efficit jugum fortunæ jugum amicitiæ
Omnis medecina Innouatio

Folio 84, front—continued.

Auribus mederi difficillimum.

Suspitio fragilem fidem soluit fortem incendit

Pauca tamen suberunt priscæ vestigia fraudis

Dulce et decorum est pro patria mori

Mors et fugacem persequitur virum.

Danda est hellebori multo pars maxima avar [is]

Folio 84, back.

COMERSATE

Minerall wytts strong poyson and they be not corrected

aquexar.

Ametallado fayned inameled.

Totum est majus sua parte against factions and priuate profite

Galens compositions not paracelsus separations

Full musike of easy ayres withowt strange concordes and discordes

In medio non sistit uirtus

FOURMES

Totem est quod superest

A stone withowt foyle

A whery man that lookes one way and pulls another

Ostracisme

Mors in Olla poysonings

Fumos uendere.

Folio 85, front.

Dec. 5, 1594.

Promus

// Suauissima vita indies meliorem fierj

The grace of God is woorth a faire

Mors in olla **F**

// No wise speech thowgh easy and voluble.

Notwithstanding his dialogues (of one that giueth life to his speach by way of quæstion. **T**

He can tell a tale well (of those cowrtly giftes of speach w[ch.] are better in describing then in consydering **F**

A goode Comediante **T** (of one that hath good grace in his speach

(To commend Judgments.

// (To comend sense of law).

// (Cunyng in the humors of persons but not in the
// condicons of actions

Stay a littell that we make an end the sooner. **A**

// A fooles bolt is soone shott

His lippes hang in his light. **A. T**

// Best we lay a straw hear

A myll post thwitten to a pudding pricke **T**

// One swallo maketh no sumer

L'Astrologia e vera ma l' astrologuo non sj truoua

// Hercules pillers non vltrâ. **T**

// He had rather haue his will then his wyshe. **T**

// Well to forgett

Make much of yourselfe

Folio 85, front—continued.

Wyshing yow all &c and myself occasion to doe yow servyce

// I shalbe gladd to vnderstand your newes but none
// rather then some ouerture whearin I may doe
// yow service

// Ceremonyes and green rushes are for strangers **T**

How doe yow? They haue a better quęstion in cheap side w[t] lak ye

// Poore and trew. Not poore therefore not trew **T**

Folio 85, back.

Tuque Inuidiosa vestustas. **T**

Licentia sumus omnes deteriores. **T**

Qui dat nivem sicut lanam **T**

Lilia agri non laborant neque nent **T**

Mors omnia solvit **T**

// A quavering tong.

like a cuntry man that curseth the almanach. **T**

Ecce duo gladij hic. **T**

Amajore ad minorem. **T**

In circuitu ambulant impij **T**

Exijt sermo inter fratres quod discipulus iste non moritur **T**

Omne majus continet in se mjnus **T**

Sine vlla controuersia quod minus est majore benedic . . . **T**

She is light she may be taken in play **T**

He may goe by water for he is sure to be well landed **T**

// Small matters need sollicitacion great are remembred of themselues

The matter goeth so slowly forward that I haue almost forgott it my self so as I maruaile not if my frendes forgett

Not like a crabb though like a snaile

Honest men hardly chaung their name. **T**

The matter thowgh it be new (if that be new w[ch.] hath been practized in like case thowgh not in this particular

I leaue the reasons to the parties relacions and the consyderacion of them to your wysdome

Folio 86, front.

I shall be content my howrs intended for service leaue me in liberty

// It is in vayne to forbear to renew that greef by speach wch. the want of so great a comfort must needes renew.

// As I did not seeke to wynne your thankes so your courteous acceptacion deserueth myne

// The vale best discouuereth the hill **T.**

// Sometymes a stander by seeth more than a plaier **T.**

The shortest foly is the best. **T.**

// I desire no secrett newes but the truth of comen newes. **T.**

Yf the bone be not trew[1] sett it will neuer be well till it be broken. **T.**

// Cheries and newes fall price soonest. **T.**

You vse the lawyers fourme of pleading **T.**

// The difference is not between yow and me but between your proffite and my trust

// All is not in years some what is in howres well spent. **T.**

// Offer him a booke **T**

// Why hath not God sent yow my mynd or me your means.

// I thinke it my dowble good happ both for the obteynyng and for the mean.

// Shutt the doore for I mean to speak treason **T.**

I wysh one as fytt as I am vnfitt

I doe not onely dwell farre from neighbors but near yll neighbors. **T**

---

1 'well' has been struck out

Folio 86, front—continued.

// As please the paynter **T.**

Receperunt mercedem suam. **T.**

Secundum fidem vestram fiet vobis

Ministerium meum honorificabo

Folio 86, back.

Beati mortuj qui moriuntur in domino
Detractor portat Diabolum in linguâ **T**
frangimur heu fatis inquit ferimurque procellâ
Nunc ipsa vocat res
Dij meliora pijs erroremque hostibus illum
Aliquisque malo fuit vsus in illo
Vsque adeo latet vtilitas
Et tamen arbitrium quęrit res ista duorum.
Vt esse phębi dulcius lumen solet
Jam jam cadentis
Velle suum cuique est nec voto viuitur vno
Who so knew what would be dear
Nead be a marchant but a year.
Blacke will take no other hew
He can yll pipe that wantes his vpper lip
Nota res mala optima
Balbus balbum rectius intelligit
L' agua va al mar
A tyme to gett and a tyme to loose
Nec dijs nec viribus ęquis
Vnum pro multis dabitur caput
Mitte hanc de pectore curam
Neptunus ventis impleuit vela secundis.
A brayne cutt with facettes **T**
T Yow drawe for colors but it prooueth contrarie
T Qui in paruis non distinguit in magnis labitur.
Every thing is subtile till it be conceyued

Folio 87, front.

That y^{t}. is forced is not forcible
More ingenious then naturall
Quod longè jactum est leviter ferit
Doe yow know it? Hoc solum scio quod nihil scio
I know it? so say many
Now yow say somewhat.$_s$. euen when yow will; now yow begynne to conceyue I begynne to say.
What doe yow conclude vpon that? etiam tentas
All is one.$_s$. Contrariorum eadam est ratio.
Repeat your reason.$_s$. Bis ac ter pulchra.
Hear me owt.$_s$. you were neuer in.
Yow iudg before yow vnderstand.$_s$. I iudg as I vnderstand.
You goe from the matter.$_s$. But it was to folow yow.
Come to the poynt.$_s$. why I shall not find yow thear
Yow doe not vnderstand y^{e} poynt.$_s$. for if I did.
Let me make an end of my tale.$_s$. That which I will say will make an end of it
Yow take more then is graunted.$_s$.
you graunt lesse then is prooued
Yow speak colorably.$_s$. yow may not say truly.
That is not so by your fauour.$_s$. But by my reason it is so

Folio 87, back.

It is so I will warrant yow.,. yow may warrant me but I thinke I shall not vowche yow

Awnswere directly.,. yow mean as you may direct me

Awnswere me shortly.,. yea that yow may coment vpon it.

The cases will come together.,. It wilbe to fight then.

Audistis quia dictum est antiquis

Secundum hominem dico

Et quin[1] non novit talia?

Hoc prætexit nomine culpa

Et fuit in toto notissima fabula cęlo

Quod quidam facit

Nec nihil neque omnia sunt quæ dicit

Facetè nunc demum nata ista est oratio

Qui mal intend pis respond

Tum decujt cum sceptra dabas

En hæc promissa fides est?

Proteges eos in tabernaculo tuo à contradictione linguarum.

πρὶν το φρονεὶν καταφρονειν επισтασαι

Sicut audiuimus sic vidimus

Credidj propter quod locutus sum.

Quj erudit derisorem sibj injuriam facit

Super mjrarj cęperunt philosopharj

NOTE.—[1] 'Quin,' this may be 'quis.'

Folio 88, front.

Prudens cęlat scientiam stultus proclamat stultitiam

Quęrit derisor sapientiam nec invenit eam.

Non recipit stultus verba prudentię nisi ea dixeris quæ sunt in corde ejus

Lucerna Dej spiraculum hominis

Veritatem eme et noli vendere

Melior claudus in via quam cursor extra viam.

The glory of God is to conceale a thing and the glory of man is to fynd owt a thing.

Melior est finis orationis quam principium.

Injtium verborum ejus stultitia et novissimum oris illius pura insania

Verba sapientium sicut aculej et vebut clavj in altum defixj.

Quj potest capere capiat

Vos adoratis quod nescitis

Vos nihil scitis

Quod est veritas.

Quod scripsj scripsj

Nolj dicere rex Judęorum sed dicens se regem Judęorum

Virj fratres liceat audacter dicere apud vos

Quod uult seminator hic verborum dicere

Folio 88, back.

Multę te literę ad Insaniam redigunt.
Sapientiam loquimur inter perfectos
Et Justificata est sapientia a filijs suis.
Scientia inflat charitas ędificat
Eadem vobis scribere mihi non pigrum vobis autem necessarium
Hoc autem dico vt nemo vos decipiat in sublimitate sermonum.
Omnia probatę quod bonum este tenete
Fidelis sermo
Semper discentes et nunquam ad scientiam veritatis pervenientes
Proprius ipsorum prophęta
Testimonium hoc verum est
Tantam nubem testium.
Sit omnis homo velox ad audiendum tardus ad loquendum.
Error novissimus pejor priore.
Quęcunque ignorant blasphemant
Non credimus quia non legimus
Facile est vt quis Augustinum vincat viderit vtrum veritate an clamore.
Bellum omnium pater
De nouueau tout est beau
De saison tout est bon
Dj danarj di senno et di fede
Ce nè manca che tu credj
Di mentira y saqueras verdad

Folio 89, front.

Magna Civitas magna solitudo
light gaines make heuy purses
He may be in my paternoster indeed
But sure he shall neuer be in my Creed
Tanti causas sciat illa furosis
What will yow?
For the rest
It is possible
Not the lesse for that
Allwaies provyded
Yf yow stay thear
for a tyme
will yow see
what shalbe the end.
Incident
Yow take it right
All this while
Whear stay we?
That agayne.
I find that straunge
Not vnlike
Yf that be so
What els
Nothing lesse
Yt cometh to that
Hear yow faile
To meet with that
Bear with that
And how now

prima facie.
more or less.
It is bycause
quasi verò
Best of all

Folio 89, front—continued.

Of grace
as if
let it not displease yow
Yow putt me in mynd
I object, I demaund I distinguish etc.
A matter not in question
few woordes need
much may be said.
yow haue
well offred.
The mean the tyme
All will not serue
Yow haue forgott nothing.
Causa patet
Tamen quære.
Well remembred
I arreste yow thear
I cannot thinke that
Discourse better
I was thinking of that
I come to that
That is iust nothing
Peraduenture Interrogatory.
Se then how (for much lesse

NOTE.—This folio is written in three columns. The first two are printed on page 209, and this page forms the third column. The first line, "Of grace," is written opposite the sixth line on page 209, "What will yow?"

Folio 89, back.

Non est apud aram Consultandem.
Eumenes litter
Sortj pater ęquus vtrique
Est quoddam [*sic*] prodire tenus si non datur vltrâ.
Quem si non tenuit magnis tamen excidit ausis
Conamur tenues grandia
Tentantem majora ferè præsentibus ęquum.
Da facilem cursum atque audacibus annue ceptis
Neptunus ventis implevit vela secundis
Crescent illæ crescetis Amores
Et quæ nunc ratio est impetus ante fuit
Aspice venturo lætentur vt omnia sęclo
In Academijs discunt credere
Vos adoratis quod nescitis
To gyue Awthors thear due as yow gyue Tyme his dew w.ch is to discouuer troth.
Vos græci semper pueri
Non canimus surdis respondent omnia syluæ
populus volt decipi
Scientiam loquimur inter perfectos
Et Justificata est sapientia a filijs suis
Pretiosa in oculis domini mors sanctorum ejus
Fęlix qui potuit rerum cognoscere causas.
Magistratus virum iudicat.
Da sapienti occasionem et addetur ej sapienta
Vitę me redde priorj
I had rather know then be knowne

Folio 90, front.

Orpheus in syluis inter Delphinas Arion

Inopem me copia fecit.

An instrument in tunyng

A yowth sett will neuer be higher.

like as children doe w$^{th.}$ their babies when they haue plaied enowgh w$^{th.}$ them they take sport to undoe them.

Faber quisque fortunæ suæ

Hinc errores multiplices quod de partibus vitæ singuli deliberant de summa nemo.

Vtilitas magnos hominesque deosque efficit auxilijs quoque fauente suis.

Qui in agone contendit a multis abstinet

Quidque cupit sperat suaque illum oracula fallunt

Serpens nisi serpentem comederit non fit Draco

The Athenians holyday.

Optimi consiliarij mortuj

Cum tot populis stipatus eat

In tot populis vix vna fides

Odere Reges dicta quæ dici iubent

Nolite confidere in principibus

Et multis vtile bellum.

Pulchrorum Autumnus pulcher

Vsque adeone times quem tu facis ipse timendum.

Dux femina facti

Res est ingeniosa dare

A long wynter maketh a full ear.

Declinat cursus aurumque uolubile tollit

Romaniscult.

Vnum augurium optimum tueri patriam

Bene omnia fecit

Folio 90, back.

Et quo quenque modo fugiatque feratque laborem edocet.

Non vlla laborum o virgo nova mi facies inopinave surgit;

Omnia præcepi atque animo mecum ante peregi.

Cultus major censu

Tale of ye frogg that swelled.

Vderit vtilitas

Qui eget verseter in turbâ

While the legg warmeth the boote harmeth

Augustus rapidè ad locum leniter in loco

My father was chudd for not being a baron.

// Prowd when I may doe any man good.

I contemn few men but most thinges.

A vn matto vno & mezo

Tantęne animis cęlestibus irę

Tela honoris tenerior

Alter rixatur de lana sępe caprina

Propugnat nugis armatus scilicet vt non

Sit mihi prima fides.

Nam cur ego amicum offendam in nugis

A skulter

We haue not drunke all of one water

Ilicet obruimur numer[o].

Numbring not weighing

let them haue long mornynges that haue not good afternoones

Cowrt howres

Constancy to remayne in the same state

Folio 90, back—continued.

The art of forgetting.
Rather men then maskers.
Variam dans otium mentem
Spire lynes.

Folio 91, front.

Veruntamen vane conturbatur omnis homo
Be the day never so long at last it ringeth to even-
song.
Vita salillum.
Non possumus aliquid contra veritatem sed pro
veritate.
Sapie[n]tia quoque perseueravit mecum
Magnorum fluuiorum navigabiles fontes.
Dos est vxoria lites
Haud numine nostro
Atque animis illabere nostris
Animos nil magne laudis egentes
Magnanimj heroes nati melioribus annis
Æuo rarissima nostro
Simplicitas
Qui silet est firmus
Si nunquam fallit imago
And I would haue thowght
Sed fugit intereà fugit irreparabile temp[us]
Totum est quod superest
In a good beleef
Possunt quia posse videntur
Justitiamque omnes cupidâ de mente fugaru [nt]
Lucrificulus
Qui bene nugatur ad mensam sępe vocatur
faciunt et tędi [um finitum?] [1]
Malum bene conditum ne moveas
Be it better be it woorse
Goe yow after him that beareth the purse
Tranquillo quilibet gubernator
Nullus emptor difficilis bonum emit opsonium
Chi semina spine non vada discalzo

NOTE.—[1] This is difficult to read. It may be "faciunt et tedia funera."

Folio 91, back.

Quoniam Moses ad duritiem cordis permi [sit] vobis
Non nossem peccatum nisi per legem.
Discite Justitiam monitj
Vbj testamentum ibi necesse est mors intercedat testatoris
Scimus quia lex bona est si quis ea vtatur legitimè
Vę vobis Jurisperitj
Nec me verbosas leges ediscere nec me Ingrato voces prostituisse foro.
fixit leges pretio atque refixit
Nec ferrea Jura Insanumque forum et populi tabularia vidit
Miscueruntque novercæ non innoxia verba
Jurisconsultj domus oraculum Civitatis
now as ambiguows as oracles.
Hic clamosi rabiosa forj
Jurgia vendens improbus
Iras et verba locat
In veste varietas sit scissura non sit
Plenitudo potestatis est plenitudo tempestatis
Iliacos intrâ muros peccatur et extra
Prosperum et felix scelus virtus vocatur
Da mihi fallere da iustum sanctumque viderj.
Nil nisi turpe iuuat curę est sua cuique voluptas
Hęc quoque ab alterius grata dolore venit
Casus ne deusne
fabulęque manes

Folio 92, front.

Ille Bioneis sermonibus et sale nigro
Existimamus diuitem omnia scire recte
Queṛunt cum quâ gente cadant
Totus mu[n]dus in malingo positus
O major tandem parcas insane minori
Reall
forma dat esse
Nec fandj fictor Vlisses
Non tu plus cernis sed plus temerarius audes
    Nec tibj plus cordis sed minus oris inest.
Invidiam placare paras virtute relicta
ὁ πολλα κλεψας ολιγα δουκ εκφευξεται
Botrus oppositus Botro citius maturescit
Old treacle new losanges
Soft fire makes sweet malt.
Good to be mery and wise
Seeldome cometh the better.
He must needes swymme that is held vp by the chynne
He that will sell lawne before he can fold it
Shall repent him before he haue sold it
No man loueth his fetters thowgh they be of gold.
The nearer the church the furder from God
All is not gold that glisters
Beggers should be no chuzers
A beck is as good as a dieu vous gard.
The rowling stone neuer gathereth mosse
Better children weep then old men

Folio 92, back.

When bale is heckst boote is next.

Ill plaieng wth. short dag. (taunting replie

He that neuer clymb neuer fell

The loth stake standeth long.

Itch and ease can no man please

To much of one thing is good for nothing.

Ever spare and euer bare.

A catt may looke on a Kyng

He had need be a wyly mowse should breed in the cattes ear.

Many a man speaketh of Rob. hood that neuer shott in his bowe.

Batchelers wyues and maides children are well taught

God sendeth fortune to fooles

Better are meales many then one to mery

Many kisse the child for the nurses sake

When the head akes all the body is the woorse

When theeues fall owt trew men come to their good

An yll wynd that bloweth no man to good.

All this wynd shakes no Corn

Thear be more waies to the wood then one

Tymely crookes the Tree that will a good Camocke be

Better is the last smile then thefirst laughter.

No peny no pater noster.

Every one for himself and God for vs all

Folio 93, front.

Long standing and small offring
The catt knowes whose lippes she lickes.
As good neuer a whitt as neuer the better.
fluvius quæ procul sunt irrigat.
As far goeth the pilgrymme as the post.
Cura esse quod audis
Εργα νεων βουλαι δε μεσων ευχαι δε γεροντων
Taurum tollet qui vitulum sustulerit
Lunæ radijs non maturescit Botrus
Nil profuerit Bulbus; ye potado will doe no good.
Dormientis rete trahit The sleeping mans nett draweth.
ijsdem è literis efficitur Tragędia et Comedia
Tragedies and Comedies are made of one Alphabett.
Good wyne needes no bush.
Heroum filij noxæ
The sonnes of demy goddes demy men.
Alia res sceptrum alia plectrum
fere danides[1]
Abore dejectâ quivis ligna colligit.
The hasty bytch whelpes a blind lytter.
Priscis credendum
We must beleeue the wytnesses are dead
Thear is no trusting a woman nor a tapp

NOTE.—[1] This is difficult to read. It may be "fero danid es."

Folio 93, back.

Not onely y^e^. Spring but the Michelmas Spring

Virj iurejurandi pueri talis fallendj

Ipsa dies quandoque parens quandoque noverca est

Vbj non sis qui fueris non esse cur velis viuere.

Compendiaria res improbitas

It is in action as it is in wayes; comonly the nearest is the fowlest

Lachrimâ nil citius arescit

woorke when God woorkes.

A shrewd turn comes vnbidden.

Hirundines sub eodem tecto ne habeas.

A thorn is gentle when it is yong.

Aut regem aut fatuum nasci oportet (of a free jester.

Exigua res est ipsa Justitia

Quæ non posuistj ne tollas

Dat veniam coruis vexat Censura columbas

Lapsa lingua verum dicit

The toung trippes vpon troth

The evill is best that is lest [best?] knowen.

A mercury cannot be made of every wood (bvt priapus may

Princes haue a Cypher

Anger of all passions beareth the age lest [best?]

One hand washeth another

Iron sharpeth against Iron.

Folio 94, front.

Eyther bate conceyte or putt to strength

faciunt et sphaceli Immunitatem.

He may be a fidler that cannot be a violine

Milke the staunding Cowe. Why folowe yow the flyeng.

He is the best prophete that telleth the best fortune

Garlike and beans

like lettize like lips

Mons cum monte non miscetur

Hilles meet not

A northen man may speake broad.

Hæsitantia Cantoris Tussis

No hucking Cator buyeth good achates.

Spes alit exules.

Romanus sedendo vincit.

Yow must sowe wth. the hand not wth. the baskett

Mentiuntur multa cantores (few pleasing speches true

It is no^{th} if it be in verse

Leonis Catulum ne alas

He cowrtes a fury

Dij laneos habent pedes (They leaue no prynt.

The weary ox setteth stronger

A mans customes are the mowldes whear his fortune is cast

Folio 94, back.

Beware of the vinegar of sweet wyne
Adoraturj sedeant[1]
To a foolish people a preest possest
The packes may be sett right by the way
It is the Cattes nature and the wenches fault.
Cœnę fercula nostrę
Mallem conviuis quam placuisse cocis.
Al Confessor medico è aduocato
Non si de tener [tena?] il ver celato
Assaj ben balla a chi fortuna suona
A yong Barber and an old phisicion
Buon vin Cattiua testa dice il griego
Buon vin fauola lunga
good watch chazeth yll aduenture
Campo rotto paga nuoua
Better be martyr then Confessor
L' Imbassador no porta pena
Bella botta non ammazza vecello.
A tender finger maketh a festred sore
A catt will neuer drowne if she see the shore.
Qui a teme [temor?] a lie
He that telleth tend [tond?] lyeth is eyther a foole himself or he to whome he telles them
Che posce a [ci?] Canâ pierde piu che guadagna.

NOTE.—[1] "Sedeant." This word is doubtful. It may be "tedeant," "te deum" is not an impossible reading.

Folio 95, front.

Ramo curto vindimi lunga
Tien l'amico tuo con viso suo.
Gloria in the end of the salme
An asses trott and a fyre of strawe dureth not
Por mucho madrugar no amanece mas ayna
Erly rising hasteneth not y^{e}. morning.
Do yra el Buey que no are?
Mas vale buena quexa que mala paga
Better good pleint then yll pay
He that pardons his enemy the amner shall haue his goodes
Chi offendi maj perdona
He that resolues in hast repentes at leasure
A dineros pagados brazos quebrados.
Mas uale bien de lexos que mal de cerca.
El lobo & la vulpeja son todos d'vna conseja
No haze poco quien tu mal echa a otro (oster before
El buen suena, el mal buela.
At the trest of the yll the lest
Di mentira y sagueras verdad
Tell a lye to knowe a treuth
La oveja mansa mamma su madre y agena
En fin la soga quiebra por el mas delgado.
Quien ruyn es en su villa ruyn es en Sevilla
Quien no da nudo pierde punto
Quien al Ciel escupe a la cara se le buelve
Covetousenesse breakes the sacke
Dos pardales à tua espiga haze mala ligua

Folio 95, back.

Quien ha las hechas ha las sospechas.
La muger que no vera no haze larga tela
Quien a las hechas ha las sospechas.
Todos los duelos con pan son buenos.
El mozo por no saber, y el viejo por no poder dexan las cosas pierder.
La hormiga quandose a de perder nasiente alas
De los leales se hinchen los huespitales.
Dos que se conoscan de lexos se saludan.
Bien ayrna quien mal come.
Por mejoria mi casa dexaria
Hombre apercebido medio combatido
He caries fier in one hand and water in the other
To beat the bush whi e another catches the byrd
To cast beyond the moone
His hand is on his halfpeny
As he brues so he must drinke
Both badd me God speed but neyther bad me wellcome
To bear two faces in a whood
To play cold prophett
To sett vp a candell before the devill
He thinketh his farthing good syluer

Folio 96, front.

Let them that be a cold blowe at the cold.

I haue seen as farre come as nigh

The catt would eat fish but she will not wett her foote

Jack would be a gentleman if he could speake french

Tell your cardes and tell me what yow haue wonne

Men know how the markett goeth by the markett men.

The keyes hang not all by one mans gyrdell.

While the grasse growes the horse starueth

I will hang the bell about the cattes neck.

He is one of them to whome God bedd heu

I will take myne altar in myne armes

for the mooneshyne in the water

It may ryme but it accords not

To make a long haruest for a lyttell corn

Folio 96, back.

Neyther to heavy nor to hott
Soft for dashing
Thowght is free
The deuill hath cast a bone to sett strife
To putt ones hand between the barke and the Tree
Who meddles in all thinges may shoe the gosling
Let the catt wynke and lett the mowse runne
He hath one pointe of a good haulke he is handy
The first poynt of a faulkener to hold fast
Ech finger is a thumb
Owt of Gods blessing into the warme sune.
At eve[r]y dogges barke to awake
A lone day
My self can tell best where my shoe wringes me
A cloke for the Rayne
To leap owt of the frieng pan into the fyre
Now toe on her distaff then she can spynne
To byte and whyne
The world runs on wheeles
He would haue better bread than can be made of
    whea[t]
To take hart of grace

Folio 97, front.

Thear was no more water then the shipp drewe
A man must tell yow tales and find yow ears
Haruest ears (of a busy man.
When thrift is in the feeld he is in the Towne
That he wynnes in y[e]. hundreth he louseth in the Shyre
To stumble at a strawe and leap over a bloc
To stoppe two gappes with one bush
To doe more than the preest spake of on Sunday
To throwe the hatchet after the helve
Yow would be ouer the stile before yow come at it.
Asinus avis (a foolish conjecture.
Herculis Cothurnos aptare infantj
To putt a childes leg into Hercules buskin
Jupiter orbus
Tales of Jupiter dead withowt yssue
Juxta fluuium puteum fodere
To dig a well by the Ryuer side
A ring of Gold on a swynes snowte
To help the sunne with lantornes
In ostio formosus (gratiows to shew
Myosobæ flyflappers (offyciows fellowes
Αδελφιζειν. To brother it (fayre speech
Jactare iugum To shake the yoke
When It was to salt to wash it with fresh water (when speach groweth in bi . . . to fynd taulke more gratfull

Folio 97, back.

Mira de lente

Quid ad farinas.

Quarta lunâ Natj (Hercules nativity.

Ollę amicitia.

Venus font.

Utraque nutans sententia

Hasta caduceum

The two that went to a feast both at dyner and supper neyther knowne, the one a tall the other a short man and said they would be one anothers shadowe. It was replied it fell owt fitt, for at noone the short man mowght be the long mans shadowe and at night the contrary.

A sweet dampe (a dislike of moist perfume.

Wyld tyme on the grownd hath a sent like a Cypresse chest.

Panis lapidosus grytty bread

Plutoes Helmett; secrecy Invisibility

Laconismus

Omnem vocem mittere (from inchantmentes

Tertium caput; (of one ouercharged that hath a burden upon eyther showder and the 3rd. vpon his head.

Triceps mercurius (great cunyng.

Creta notare (chaulking and colouring

Folio 98, front.

Vt phidię signum (presently allowed

Jovis sandalium; (Jupiters slipper (a man onely esteemed for nearnesse

Pennas nido majore extendere.

Hîc Rhodus Hîc Saltus (exacting demonstracion.

Atticus in portum

Divinum excipio sermonem

Agamemnonis hostia

W^th sailes and owres

To way ancre.

To keep strooke (fitt conjunctes

To myngle heauen and earth together

To stirr his curteynes (to raise his wyttes and sprites Comovere sacra

To iudg the Corne by the strawe

Domj Conjecturam facere (ὄικοθεν εικαζ [ειν]

To divine with a sive (?)

Mortuus per somnum vacabis curis (of one that interpretes all thinges to the best

Nil sacrj es (Hercules to adonis.

Plumbeo iugulare gladio (A tame argument

Locrensis bos (a mean present

Ollaris Deus. (a man respected for his profession withowt woorth in himself

In foribus Vrceus; an earthen pott in the threshold

Numerus

Folio 98, back.

To drawe of the dregges

Lightenyng owt of a payle

Durt tramped wth. bloude.

Ni pater esses

Vates secum auferat omen.

In eo ipso stas lapide vbj præco prædicat. of one that is abowt to be bowght and sold.

Lydus ostium claudit (of one that is gone away wth. his purpose.

Vtranque paginam facit An auditors booke (of one to whome both good and yll is imputed.

Non navigas noctu (of one that govern[s] himself acaso (bycause the starres which were wont to be the shipmans direction appear but in the night.

It smelleth of the lampe

You are in the same shippe

Between the hamer and the Andville

Res est in cardine

Vndarum in vinis

Lepus pro carnibus (of a man persecuted for profite and not for malice

Corpore effugere

Nunquid es saul inter prophetas

A dog in the manger

Οἰκουρος (a howsedowe a dedman.

Folio 99, front.

Officere luminibus

I may be in their light but not in their way.

Fęlicibus sunt et timestres liberj.

To stumble at the threshold

Aquilæ senectus

Of the age now they make popes of

Nil ad Parmenonis suem

Aquila in nubibus (a thing excellent but remote

Mox Sciemus melius vate

In omni fabula et Dædali execratio (of one made a party to all complaintes.

Semper tibj pendeat hamus.

Res redit ad triarios.

Tentantes ad trojam pervenere gręci

Cignea cantio

To mowe mosse (vnseasonable taking of vse or profite

Ex tripode

Ominabitur aliquis te conspecto.

He came of an egge

Leporem comedit

Folio 99, back.

H ταν η επι ταν

Dormientis rete trahit

Vita doliaris

He castes another mans chaunces.

I neuer liked proceeding vpon Articles before bookes nor betrothinges before mariages.

Lupus circa puteum chorum agit

The woolue danceth about the welle.

Spem pretio emere

Agricola semper in nouum annam diues.

To lean to a staffe of reed

fuimus Troes.

Ad vinum disertj.

To knytt a rope of sand.

Pedum visa est via

Panicus casus

Penelopes webb

σκιαμαχειν

To striue for an asses shade

Laborem serere.

Hylam inclamat.

θεομαχειν

To plowe the wyndes

Actum agere

Versuram soluere. To euade by a greater mischeef.

Bulbos quęrit (of those that looke downe

Between the mowth and the morsell

A Buskin (that will serve both legges

not an indifferent man but a dowble spye

Folio 100, front.

Chamelęon, Proteus, Euripus.

Mu[l]ta novit uulpes sed Echinus unum magnum

Semper Africa aliquid monstrj parit

Ex eodem ore calidum et frigidum.

Ex se finxit velut araneus

Laqueus laqueum cepit.

Hinc illę lachrimę; Hydrus in dolio

Dicas tria ex Curiâ (liberty vpon dispaire

Argi Collis (a place of robbing.

Older then Chaos.

Samiorum flores

A bride groomes life

Samius comatus (of one of no expectacion and great proof

Adonis gardens (thinges of great pleasure but soone fading.

Quę sub axillis fiunt.

In crastinum seria.

To remooue an old tree

Κυμακωφον (of one that fretteth and vaunteth boldnesse to vtter choler.

To bite the br[i]dle

Lesbia regula.

Vnguis in vlcere

To feed vpon musterd

In antro trophonij (of one that neuer laugheth

Arctum annulum ne gestato

Folio 100, back.

Areopagita; Scytala.

Cor ne edito.

Cream of Nectar

Promus magis quam Condus.

He maketh to deep a furrowe

Charons fares

Amazonum cantile[n]a; The Amazons song (Delicate persons.

To sow curses.

To quench fyre with oyle

Ex ipso boue lora sumere.

Mala attrahens ad se vt Cesias nubes

Pryaustę gaudes gaudium.

Bellerophontis literæ (producing lettres or evidence against a mans self

Puer glaciem.

To hold a woolf by the ears

fontibus apros, floribus austrum

Softer then the lippe of the ear

More tractable then wax

Aurem vellere.

Ηεριτριμμα; frippon

To picke owt the Ravens eyes.

Centones

Improbitas muscę (an importune that wilbe soone awnswered but straght in hand agayne

Argentangina, sylver mumpes

Lupi illum videre priores

Dorica musâ.

To looke a gyven horse in the mowth

Folio 101, front.

Vlysses pannos exuit.

fatis imputandum

Lychnobij

Terræ filius

Hoc jam et vates sciunt

Whear hartes cast their hornes

few dead byrdes fownd.

Prouolvitur ad milvios (a sickly man gladd of the spring.

Amnestia

Odi memorem compotorem.

Delius natator.

Numeris platonis obscurius

Dauus sum non Oedipus

Infixo aculeo fugere

Genuino mordere.

Ansam quærere.

Quę sunt apud inferos sermones.

Et Scellij filium abominor (of him that cannot endure the sound of a matter; from Aristocrates Scellius sonne, whome a man deuoted to a democracy said he could not abide for the nearnesse of his name to an Aristocracy.

Water from the handes (such doctrynes as are polluted by custome

Folio 101, back.

famis campus an yll horse kept
The thredd is sponne now nedes the neadle
quadratus homo. a Cube.
fenum habet in Cornu.
Armed intreaty.
Omnia secunda saltat senex.
θεων χειρες
Mopso Nisa datur
Dedecus publicum.
Riper then a mulbery.
Tanquam de Narthecio
Satis quercus ; Enowgh of Acornes.
Haile of perle.
Intus canere.
Symonidis Cantilena.
Viam qui nescit ad mare
Alter Janus.
To swyme withowt a barke
An owles egg.
Shake another tree
È terra spectare naufragia
In diem vivere
Vno die consenescere.
Πορρω διος τε Κ [α] ι κεραυνου
Servire scęnæ.
Omnium horarum homo
Spartæ servi maxime servi
Non sum ex istis heriobus (*sic*) (potentes ad nocendum

Folio 101, back—continued.

Scopæ dissolutę
Clavum clauo pellere
Extrà quęrere sese

Folio 102, front.

Cumjnj sector
Laconicę lunæ.
Coruus aquat.
Ne incalceatus in montes.
Domj Milesia
Sacra hęc non aliter constant.
Gallus insistit
Leonis vestigia quæris (ostentation with couardize
fumos vendere
Epiphillides.
Calidum mendacium optimum
Solus Currens vincit.
Vulcaneum vinclum.
Salt to water (whence it came
Canis sęviens in lapidem
Aratro iacularj.
Semel rubidus decies pallidus.
Tanto buon che ual niente
So good, as he is good for nothing.
The crowe of the bellfry.
The vinegar of sweet wyne.
En vne nuit naist vn champignon.
He hath more to doe then the ovens in Christmas.
piu doppio ch' una zevola
Il cuopre vn altare & discuopre l' altro
He will hide himself in a mowne medowe
Il se crede segnar & se da de dettj ne gli occhi
He thinkes to blesse himself and thrustes his fingers into his eyes

Folio 102, back.

He is gone like a fay withowt his head
La sopra scritta è buona
La pazzia li fa andare }
La vergogna li fa restare }
Mangia santj & caga Diauolj.
Testa digiuna, barba pasciuta.
L'asne qui porte le vin et boit l'eau
lyke an ancher that is euer in the water and will neuer learn to swyme
He doth like the ape that the higher he clymbes the more he shews his ars.
Se no va el otero a Mahoma vaya Mahoma al otero.
Nadar y nadar y ahogar a la orilla
llorar duelos agenos
Si vos sabes mucho tambien se yo mi salm[o?]
Por hazer mi miel comieron mj muxcas
Come suol d'Invierno quien sale tarde y pone presto.
Lo que con el ojo veo con el dedo lo adeuino
Hijo no tenemos y nombre lo ponemos.
Por el buena mesa y mal testamento.
Era mejor lamiendo que no mordiendo
Perro del hortelano
Despues d'yo muerto ni vinna ni huerto
Perdj mj honor hablando mal y oyendo peor
Tomar asino que me lleue y no cauallo que me derruque.

Folio 103, front.

So many heades so many wittes
Happy man happy dole
In space cometh grace
Nothing is impossible to a willing hand
Of two ylles chuze the lest.
Better to bow then to breake
Of suffrance cometh ease
Two eyes are better then one.
Leaue is light
Better vnborn then vntaught.
All is well that endes well
Of a good begynyng comes a good ending
Thinges doone cannot be vndoone
Pride will haue a fall
Some what is better then nothing
Better be envyed then pytied
Every man after his fashon
He may doe much yll ere he doe much woorse
We be but where we were
Vse maketh mastery
Loue me lyttell love me long.
They that are bownd must obey
Foly it is to spurn against the pricke
Better sitt still then rise and fall.
Might overcomes right
No smoke wth. owt some fire
Tyme tryeth troth
Make not to sorowes of one

Folio 103, back.

Thear is no good accord
whear euery one would be a lord
Saieng and doing are two thinges
Better be happy then wise
Who can hold that will away
Allwaies let leasers haue their woordes
Warned and half armed
He that hath an yll name is half hanged
Frenzy Heresy and jalousy are three
That seeldome or neuer cured be
That the ey seeth not the hart rueth not
Better comyng to the ending of a feast then to the begynyng of a fray
Yll putting a swoord in a mad mans hand
He goes farre that neuer turneth
Principium dimidium totius
Quot homines tot sententię
Suum cujque pulchrum.
Quę suprâ nos nihil ad nos
Ama tanquam osurus oderis tanquam amaturus.
Amicorum omnia communia
Vultu sępe lęditur pietas
Fortes fortuna adjuuat.
Omne tulit punctum.
In magnis et uoluisse sat est
Difficilia quę pulchra.
Tum tua res agitur paries cum proximus ardet
Et post malam segetem serendum est
Omnium rerum vicissitudo

Folio 103 back—continued.

In nil sapiendo vita jucundissima
Parturiunt montes nascetur ridiculus mus
Dulce bellum inexpertis
Naturam expellas furcâ licet vsque recurret.

Folio 104, front.

Quo semel est imbuta recens servabit odorem
Bis dat qui cito dat
Consciencia mille testes
In vino veritas
Bonæ leges ex malis moribus
Nequicquam sapit qui sibj non sapit
Summum jus summa injuria
Sera in fundo parsimonia
Optimum non nasci
Musa mihi causas memora
        Longę
Ambages sed summa sequar fastigia rerum }
Causasque innecte morandj
Incipit effari mediaque in voce resistit
Sensit enim simulata voce locutam
quæ prima exordia sumat
Hæc alternantj potior sententia visa est.
Et inextricabilis error
Obscuris vera inuolvens.
Hæ tibi erunt artes
Sic genus amborum scindit se sanguine ab vno.
Varioque viam sermone leuabat
Quid causas petis ex alto fiducia cessit
Quo tibj Diua mej
Causas nequicquam nectis inanes
        quid me alta silentia cogis
Rumpere et obductum verbis vulgare dolorem
Nequicquam patrias tentasti lubricus artes
Do quod uis et me victusque uolensque remitto

Folio 104, front—continued.

Sed scelus hoc meritj pondus et instar habet
Quæque prior nobis intulit ipse ferat
Officium fecere pium sed invtile nobis
Exiguum sed plus quam nihil illud erit
Sed lateant vires nec sis in fronte disertus
Sit tibj credibilis sermo consuetaque verba
præsens vt videare loqui

Folio 104, back.

Ille referre aliter sȩpe solebat idem
Nec uultu destrue verba tuo
Nec sua vesanus scripta poeta legat
Ars casum simulet
Quid cum legitima fraudatur litera uoce
Blæsaque fit iusso lingua coacta sono
Sed quæ non prosunt singula multa iuuant.
Sic parvis componere magna solebam
Alternis dicetis
    paulo majora canamus
Non omnes arbusta iuuant
Et argutos inter strepere anser olores.
Causando nostros in longum ducis amores
Nec tibj tam sapiens quisquam persuadeat autor
Nec sum animj dubius verbis ea vincere magnum
    quam sit et angustis hunc addere rebus honorem
Sic placet an melius quis habet suadere
Quamquam ridentem dicere verum
    quis vetat
Sed tamen amoto quæramus seria ludo
Posthabuj tamen illorum mea seria ludo
O imitatores seruum pecus
Quam temere in nobis legem sancimus iniquam.
    mores sensusque repugnant
Atque ipsa vtilitas justj propè mater et ȩqui
    dummodo visum
Excutiat sibj non hic cuiquam parcit amico
Nescio quod meritum nugarum totus in illis
Num[1] quid vis occupo

NOTE.—[1] "Num" may be read as "Nunc."

Folio 104, back—continued.

Noris nos inquit doctj sumus
O te bollane cerebrj
Fęlicem aiebam tacitus.

Folio 105, front.

ridiculum acrj
Fortius et melius magnas plerunque secat res.
At magnum fecit quod verbis græca latinis }
Miscuit ô serj studiorum }
Nil ligat exemplum litem quod lite resoluit
Nimirum insanus paucis videatur eo quod }
Maxima pars hominum morbo laborat eodem }
Neu si vafer vnus et alter
Insidiatorem præroso fugerit hamo
Aut spem deponas aut artem illusus omittas
gaudent prænomine molles }
auriculæ }
Renuis tu quod jubet alter
Qui variare cupit rem prodigaliter unam.
Et adhuc sub judice lis est.
Proijcit ampullas et sesquipedalia verba
Quid dignum tanto feret hic promissor hiatu
Atque ita mentitur sic veris falsa remittet
tantum series juncturaque pollet
Tantum de medio sumptis accedit honoris
Ergo fungar vice cotis acutum }
Reddere quę possit ferrum exors ipsa secandj }
Hæc placuit semel hæc decies repetita placebit
Fas est et ab hoste docerj
Vsque adeo quod tangit idem est tamen vltima [distans.
Quis furor auditos inquit præponere visis
Pro munere poscimus vsum
Inde retro redeunt idemque retexitur ordo
Nil tam bonum est quin male narrando possit deprauarier

Folio 105, back.

Furor arma ministrat
Pulchrumque morj succurrit in armis
Aspirat primo fortuna laborj
Facilis jactura sepulchrj
Cedamus phœbo et monitj meliora sequamu[r]
Fata uiam invenient
Degeneres animos timor arguit
Viresque acquirit eundo
Et caput inter nubila condit
Et magnas territat vrbes
Tam ficti prauique tenax quam nuntia verj
Gaudens et pariter facta atque infecta canebat
Nusquam tuta fides
Et oblitos famæ meliori amantes
Varium et mutabile semper
    Fęmina
Furens quid fęmina possit
Quo fata trahunt retrahuntque sequamur
Quicquid id est superanda est omnis fortun[a] ferendo
Tu ne cede malis sed contrâ audentior i[to]
Hoc opus hic labor est
Nullj fas casto sceleratum insistere li[men]
Discite justitiam monitj.
Quisque suos patimur manes
Neu patrię validat[1] in viscera vertite vires
Verique effęta senectus.
At patiens operum paruoque assueta iuuen[tus]
Juno vires animumque ministrat
Nescia mens hominum fatj sortisque futur[æ]
Et servare modum rebus sublata secund[is]

NOTE.—[1] "Validat" may be read "Validas."

Folio 106, front.

Spes sibi quisque
Nec te vllius violentia vincat
Respice res bello varias
Credidimus lachrimis an et hæ simulare docentur
Hę quoque habent artes quaque iubentur eunt
Quæcunque ex merito spes venit ęqua venit
Simplicitas digna fauore fuit
Exitus acta probat careat successibus opto
Quisquis ab euentu facta notanda putet.
Ars fit vbj a teneris crimen condiscitur annis
Jupiter esse pium statuit quodcunque iuuaret
Non honor est sed onus
Si qua voles apte nubere nube parj
Perdere posse sat est si quem iuuat ista potestas.
Terror in his ipso major solet esse periclo
Quæque timere libet pertimuisse pudet
An nescis longas regibus esse manus
Vtilis interdum est ipsis injuria passis
Fallitur augurio spes bona sępe suo
Quæ fecisse iuuat facta referre pudet
Consilium prudensque animj sententia jurat
Et nisi judicij vincula nulla valent
Sin abeunt studia in mores
Illa verecundis lux est præbenda puellis
Qua timidus latebras speret habere pudor
Casta est quam nemo rogauit
Quj non vult fierj desidiosus amet
Gratia pro rebus merito debetur inemptis
Quem metuit quisque perisse cupit

Folio 106, back.

A late promus of formularies
and elegancies

Synanthr
Synanthropy

Folio 107, front.

He that owt leaps his strength standeth not

He keeps his grownd; Of one that speaketh certenly & pertinently

He lighteth well; of one that concludeth his speach well

Of speaches digressive; This goeth not to the ende of the matter; from the lawyers.

for learnyng sake.

Mot. of the mynd explicat in woords implicat in thowghts

I iudg best implicat in thowg. or of trial or mark bycause of swiftnes collocat. & differe & to make woords sequac.

Folio 107, back.

[Blank]

Folio 108, front.

Vpon Impatience of Audience

Verbera sed audi.

Auribus mederj difficillimum.

Noluit Intelligere vt benè ageret

The ey is the gate of the affection, but the ear of the vnderstanding

The fable of the syrenes

Placidasque viri deus obstruit aures

Vpon quęstion to reward evill wth. evill

Noli æmularj in malignantibus

Crowne him wth tols (?)

Nil malo quam illos similes esse suj et me mej

Cum perverso perverteris; lex talionis

Yow are not for this world

Tanto buon cheval niente

Vpon quęstion whether a man should speak or forbear speach

Quia tacuj inveterauerunt ossa mea (speach may now & then breed smart in ye. flesh; but keeping it in goeth to ye bone.

Credidi propter quod locutus sum.

Obmutuj et humiliatus sum siluj etaim a bonis et dolor meus renouatus est.

Obmutuj et non aperuj os meum quoniam tu fecistj

It is goddes doing.

Posuj custodiam Orj meo cum consisteret peccator aduersum me.

Ego autem tanquam surdus non audiebam et tanquam mutus non aperiens os suum

Folio 108, back.

Benedictions and maledictions

Et folium eius non defluet
Mella fluant illj ferat
et rubus asper amonium

Abominacion

Dij meliora pijs
Horresco referens

Folio 109, front.

Per otium To any thing impertinent.

Speech y[t] hangeth not together nor is concludent. Raw sylk; sand.

Speech of good & various wayght but not neerely applied; A great vessell y[t] cannot come neer land.

Of one y[t]. rippeth things vp deepely. He shooteth to high a compass to shoote neere.

Y[e]. law at Twicknam for mery tales

Synanthropie

Folio 109, back.

[Blank]

Folio 109c, front.

[Blank]

Folio 109d, back.

Synanthropie

Folio 110, front.

Play.

The syn against y^e^. holy ghost termd in zeal by one of y^e^. fathers

Cause of Oths; Quarells; expence & vnthriftynes; ydlenes & indisposition of y^e^. mynd to labors.

Art of forgetting; cause of society acquaintance familiarity in frends; neere & ready attendance in servants; recreation & putting of melancholy; Putting of malas curas & cupiditates.

Games of Actiuity & passetyme; *sleight* of Act . of strength quicknes; quick . of ey hand; legg, the whole mocion; strength of arme; legge; *Of Activity of sleight.*

Of passetyme onely; of hazard, of play mixt

Of hazard; meere hazard Cunnyng in making yor. game; Of playe: exercise of attention;

of memory; of Dissimulacion; of discrecion;

Of many hands or of receyt; of few; of quick returne tedious; of præsent iudgment; of vncerten yssue.

Seuerall playes or Ideas of play.

Frank play; wary play, venturous not venturous quick slowe;

Oversight Dotage Betts Lookers on Judgment groome porter; Christmas; Invention for hunger Oddes; stake; sett;

He that folowes his losses & giueth soone over at wynnings will never gayne by play

Ludimus incauti studioque aperimur ab ipso

Folio 110, front—continued.

He that playeth not the begynnyng of a game well at tick tack & y^e^. later end at yrish shall never wynne

Frier Gilbert

Y^e^. lott; earnest in old tyme sport now as musik owt of church to chamber

Folio 110, back.

[Blank]

Folio 111.

[Blank]

Folio 112, front.

good morow
Good swear[1]
Good trauaile
good hast
good matens
good betymes; bonum manè
bon iouyr. Bon iour; (bridgrome.)
good day to me & good morow to yow.
I haue not sayd all my prayers till I haue bid yow
good morow.
Late rysing fynding a bedde,
early risinge, summons to ryse
Diluculo surgere saluberrimum est.
Surge puer mane sed noli surgere vanè.
Yow will not rise afore yor. betters
(y^{e}. sonne.
Por mucho madrugar no amanece mas ayna.
Qui a bon voisin a bon matin
(lodged next;
Stulte quid est somnus gelidæ nisi mortis imago
Longa quiescendi tempora fata dabunt.
Albada; golden sleepe.
early vp & neuer ye neere.
The wings of y^{e}. mornyng.
The yowth & spring of y^{e}. day
The Cock; The Larke.
Cowrt howres.

NOTE.—[1] "Swear," this may be read "Sweat."

Folio 112, front—continued.

Constant; abedd when yow are bedd; & vp when yow are vp.

Trew mens howres.

Is this your first flight × I doe not as byrds doe for I fly owt of my feathers z Is it not a fayre one

Sweet, fresh of y^e^. mornyng.

I pray god your early rysing doe yow no hurt; Amen when I vse it.

I cannot be ydle vp as yow canne.

Yow could not sleep for your yll lodging; I cannot gett owt of my good lodginge.

Yow have an alarum in your head

Block heads & clock heads.

There is Law against lyers a bedde.

Yow haue no warrant to ly a bedde

Synce yow are not gott vp turn vp.

Hott cocckles withowt sands

god night

Well to forgett;

I wish yow may so well sleepe as yow may not fynd yor yll lodging.

Note.—This folio is written in two columns. The second column begins with the line, "I pray god your early rysing."

Folio 112, back.

[Blank]

Folio 113, front.

[Blank]

Folio 113, back.

fourmes & elegancyes.

Folio 114, front.

Formularies Promus 27 Jan. 1595.

Against conceyt of difficulty or impossibility vt s[upra]	Tentantes ad Trojam peruenere græcj atque omnia pertentare	Es. conceyt of Impossibilities & Imaginations ad id.
Abstinence negatiues	Qui in agone contendit a multis abstinet.	Ess. indearing generalities & præcepts
vt s[upra]	All the Commaundments negatiue saue two	ad id. ad id.
Curious; Busy without jugment good direction	Parerga; mouente sed nil promouentes operosities, nil ad summam.	ad id. and extenuating deuises & particulars.
vt s [upra]	Claudus in via	ad id.
[1] Direction generall.	to giue the grownd in bowling.	
vt sup[ra]	Like tempring with phisike a good diett much better.	ad id.
Zeal affection alacrity	Omni possum in eo qui me confortat	Idea. zeal & good affection y[e]. e.
vt s[upra]	Possunt quia posse videntur	ad id.
vt s[upra]	Exposition of Not Overweenning but ouerwilling.	ad id.
vt s[upra]	Goddes presse; Voluntaries	ad id.
detraction	Chesters wytt to depraue & otherwise not wyse	[2]s. P. s J.
Hast impatience	In actions as in wayes the nearest y[e]. fowlest	Ind my stay

NOTES.—[1] The side note "Direction generall" has been struck out in the MS
[2] s. P. s. J. may be read s R s. f.

Folio 114, back.

[Blank]

Folio 115, front.

[Blank]

Folio 115, back.

ffrancys Dalle

fragments of Elegancyes

Folio 116, front.

// Quod adulationis nomine dicitur bonum quod obtrectationis malum.

Cujus contrarium majus; majus aut priuatio cujus minus animis. ‡

// Cujus opus et uirtus majus majus cujus minus minus

// quorum cupiditates majores aut meliores,

// quorum scientiæ aut artes honestiores.

// quod uir melior eligeret vt injuriam potius pati quam facere.

// quod manet melius quam quod transit.

// quorum quis autor cupit esse bonum, cujus horret malum.

// quod quis amico cupit facere bonum quod inimico malum.

// Diuturniora minus diuturnis

Conjugata

// quod plures eligunt potius quam quod pauciores.

// quod controuertentes dicunt bonum perinde ac omnes quod scientes et potentes, quod judicantes.

// Quorum præmia majora, majora bona, quorum mulctæ majores, majora mala.

Quæ confessis et tertijs majoribus majora.

// quod ex multis constat magis bonum cum multi articulj bonj dissectj magnitudinem præ se ferunt

Natiua ascitis.

// Qua supra ætatem præter occasionem aut oportunitate præter naturam tocj præter conditionem temporis præter naturam personæ vel instrumenti vel iuuamenti majora quam quæ secundum.

Folio 116, back.

// quæ in grauiore tempore vtilia vt in morbo senectute
// aut aduersis.
// Ex duobus medijs quod propinquius est fruj
// Quæ tempore futuro et vltimo quia sequens tempus
// evacuat præterita
Antiqua novis noua antiquis
Consueta nouis noua consuetis
// quod ad veritatem magis quam ad opinionem Ejus
// [1]antè. quæ ad opinionem pertinet, ratio est ac
// modus, quod quis sj clam fore putaret non
// eligeret
// Polychreston vt diuitiæ, robur, potentia, facultates
// animj
Ex duobus quod tertio ęquali adjunctum majus ipsa[2]
reddit
Quæ non latent cum adsunt, quam quæ latere
possunt majora.
// quod magis ex necessitate vt oculus vnus lusco
// quod expertus facile reliquit
// quod quis cogitur facere malum
// quod sponte fit bonum
// quod bono confesso redimitur

NOTES.—[1] "ante," this may be read "autè" = "autem." [2] "ipsa" this may be read "ipsû" = "ipsum."

Folio 117, front.

In deliberatives and electives

Folio 117, back.

Cujus excusatio paratior est vel venia indulta magis minus malum.

Folio 118, front.

Melior est oculorum visio quam animj progressio

// Spes in dolio remansit sed non vt antedotum sed vt major morbus

Spes omnis in futuram vitam consumendus sufficit præsentibus bonis purus sensus.

Spes vigilantis somnium; vitæ summa breuis spem nos uetat inchoare longam.

// Spes facit animos leues timidos inęquales peregrinantes

// Vidi ambulantes sub sole cum adolescente secundo qui consurget post eum.

// Imaginationes omnia turbant, timores multiplicant voluptates corrumpunt.

// Anticipatio timores[1] salubris ob inventionem remedij spei institit[2]

Imminent futuro, ingrati in præteritum semper adolescentes

Vitam sua sponte fluxam magis fluxam reddimus per continuationes spe

Præsentia erunt futura non contra

NOTES.—[1] "Timores" may be read "timoris." [2] "Institit" = insistit.

Folio 118, back.

[Blank]

Folio 119, front.

[Blank]

Folio 119, back.

[Blank]

Folio 120, front.

The fallaxes of y^e^. 3 and y^e^. assurance of Erophil. to fall well euery waye
Watry impressions, fier elementall fier æthereall.
Y^e^. memory of that is past cannot be taken from him.
All 3 in purchaze nothing in injoyeng.

Folio 120, back.

[Blank]

Folio 121, front.

[Blank]

Folio 121, back.

[Blank]

Folio 122, front.

// Quod inimicis nostris gratum est ac optabile vt *nobis* eveniat malum, quod molestiæ et terrorj est bonum.

Metuo danaos et dona ferentes

Hoc Ithacus velit et magno mercentur Atridæ.

Both parties haue wyshed battaile

The Launching of y^e^. Imposture by him that intended murder.

Conciliam homines mala. a forein warre to appeas parties at home

// Quod quis sibj tribuit et sumit bonum, quod in alium transfert malum

non tam inuidiæ impertiendæ quam laudis communicandæ gratia loquor.

// Quod quis facile impertit minus bonum quod quis paucis et grauatim impertit majus bonum

Te nunc habet ista secundum.

// Quod per ostentationem fertur bonum, quod per excusationem purgatur malum.

// Nescio quid peccati portet hæc purgatio.

// Cuj sectæ diuersæ quæ sibj quæque præstantiam vendicat secundas tribuit melior singulis

// Secta Academicæ quam Epicureus et stoicus sibi tantum postponit

// Neutrality.

Folio 122, back.

// Cujus exuperantia vel excellentia melior ejus et
// genus melius.

Bougeon de mars. enfant de paris.

Whear they take
Some thinges of lyttell valew but excellencye
Some more indifferent and after one sort.

// In quo periculosius erratur melius eo in quo erratur
// minore cum periculo.

// Quod rem integram seruat, melius eo a quo receptus
// non est potestatem enim donat potestas autem
// bonum

The tale of the frogges that were wyshed by one in a drowth to repayre to the bottome of a well, ay (?) but if water faile thear how shall we gett vp agayne

// Quod polychrestum est melius quam quod ad vnum
// refertur ob incertos casus humanos.

// Cujus contrarium priuatio malum bonum cujus
// bonum malum.

// In quo non est satietas neque nimium melius eo in
// quo satietas est

// In quo vix erratur melius eo in quo error procliuis

// Finis melior ijs quæ ad finem;

// Cujus causa sumptus facti et labores toleratj
// bonum; si vt euitetur malum,

// Quod habet riuales et de quo homines contendunt
// bonum; de quo non est contentio malum.

Differ. inter fruj et acquirere.

Folio 123, front.

// Quod laudatur et prædicatur bonum quod occultatur
// et uituperatur malum.

// Quod etiam inimicj et maleuoli laudant valde bonum,
// quod etiam amicj reprehendunt magnum malum.

Quod consulto et per meliora judicia proponitur majus bonum.

// Quod sine mixtura malj melius quam quod refractum
// et non syncerum.

Possibile et facile bonum quod sine labore et paruo tempore cont[ra] malum

Bona confessa jucundum sensu; comparatione.

Honor; voluptas;

Vita

bona ualetudo

suauia objecta sensuum;

Inducunt tranquillum sensum virtutes ob securitatem et contemptum rerum humanarum; facultates animj et rerum gerendarum ob spem et metum subigendum; et diuiti . . .

Ex aliena opinione; laus.

Quæ propria sunt et minus communicata; ob honor.

quæ continent, vt animalia vt plantæ et amplius; sed id amplius potest esse malj.

Congruentia, ob raritatem et genium et proprietatem vt in familijs et professionibus

Quæ sibj deesse quis putat licet sint exigua

Folio 123, back.

ad quæ naturâ procliues sunt
quæ nemo abjectus capax est vt faciat
Majus et continens minore et contento
Ipsum quod suj causa eligitur
quod omnia appetunt.
quod prudentiam adepti eligunt
quod efficiendi et custodiendj vim habet.
Cuj res bonæ sunt consequentes.
maximum maximo ipsum ipsis; vnde exuperant . . .
quæ majoris bonj conficientia sunt ea majora sunt bona.
quod propter se expetendum eo quod propter alios
Fall. in diuersis generibus et proportionibus
Finis non finis
Minus indigens eo quod magis indiget quod paucioribus et facilioribus indiget
quoties ho (*sic*) sine illo fierj no (*sic*) potest, illud sine hoc fierj potest illud melius
principium non principio; finis autem et principium antitheta; non majus videtur principium quia primum est in opere; contra finis quia primum in mente; de perpetratore et consiliario.
Rarum copiosis honores; mutton venison
Copiosum varit vsu: optimum aqua
difficiliora, facilioribus }
faciliora, difficilioribus }

Folio 124, front.

Quod magis a necessitate vt oculus vnus lusco.

Major videtur gradus priuationis quam diminutionis

Quæ non latent cum adsunt majora quam quę latere possunt.

Quod expertus facile reliquit malum, quod mordicus tenet bonum.

In aliquibus manetur quia non datur regressus

Quæ in grauiore tempore vtilia vt in morbo senectute aduersis.

The soldier like a coreselett; bellaria, et appetitiua, redd hearing. Loue

Quod controuertentes dicunt bonum perinde ac omnes.

Sermon frequented by papists and puritans;

Matter of circumstance not of substance

boriæ penetrabile frigus adurit

Cacus oxen forwards and backwards

Not examyning.

Folio 124, back.

[Blank]

Folio 125, front.

[Blank]

Folio 125, back.

[Blank]

Folio 126, front.

Analogia Cæsaris

Verb. et clausulæ ad
exercitationem accentus
et ad gratiam sparsam
et ad suitatem

Say that; (for admitt that)

Peraventure can yow: sp̂. (what can yow)

So much there is. fr̂. (neuerthelesse)

See then how. Sp̂. (Much lesse)

Yf yow be at leasure | furnyshed etc. as perhappes yow are (in stead of are not)

For the rest (a transition concluding)

The rather bycause (contynuing anothers speach

To the end, sauing that, whereas yet (contynuance and so of all kynds

In contemplation (in consideracon)

Not præjudicing.

With this (cum hoc quod verificare vult)

Without that (absque hoc quod

It is like S[r]. etc. (putting a man agayne into his tale interrupted

Your reason

I haue been allwaies at his request;

His knowledg lieth about him

Such thoughts I would exile into into my dreames

A good crosse poynt but the woorst cinq a pase

He will never doe his tricks clean.

A proper young man and so will he be while he liues

2 of these fowre take them where yow will

I have knowne the tyme and it was not half an howre agoe

Pyonner in the myne of truth

Folio 126, front—continued.

for this tyme (when a man extends his hope or imaginacion or beleefe to farre

A mery world when such fellowes must correct (A mery world when the simplest may correct.

As please the painter

A nosce teipsum (a chiding or disgrace

Valew me not y^e^. lesse bycause I am yours.

Is it a small thing y^t^ & (cannot yow not be content

an hebraisme

What els? Nothing lesse.

It is not the first vntruth I have heard reported nor it is not ye first truth I haue heard denied.

I will prooue ×
why goe and prooue it

Minerall wytts strong poyson yf they be not corrected.

O the'

O my l. S^t^.

Beleeue it

Beleeue it not;

for a time

Mought it pleas god that fr (I would to god Neuer may it please yow

As good as the best:

I would not but yow had doone it (But shall I doe it againe

NOTE.—This folio is written in three columns. The third column begins, "It is a small thing."

Folio 126, back.

The sonne of some what Sp̂

To frime (to Sp[1]

To cherish or endear;

To vndeceyue. Sp̂ to disabuse

deliuer and vnwrapped

To discount (To Cleere)

Brazed (impudent

Brawned Seared) vnpayned.

Vuelight (Twylight) banding (factions.

Remoouing (remuant)

A third person (a broker

A nose Cutt of; tucked vp.

His disease hath certen traces)

To plaine him on

Ameled (fayned counterfett in ye best kynd

Having (?) the vpper grownd (Awthority

His resorts (his Conceyts

It may be well last for it hath lasted well

Those are great with yow y[t] are great by yow

y[e]. ayre of his behauiour; factious;

Note.—[1] "To frime (to Sp̂," this line may read, "To frime (to Suse Sp̂."

Folio 126, back—continued.

The Avenues; A back thought.

Baragan; perpetuo Juuenis

A Bonance (a Caulme

To drench to potion (to insert

Haggard insauvaged

Infistuled (made hollow with malign deales.

Folio 127, front.

[Blank]

Folio 127, back.

Cursitours lament and cry

[1]Verba interjectiua siue ad gratiam sparsam

[[1] This is an endorsement across the page.]

Folio 128, front.

Semblances or popularities of good and evill wth. their redargutions. for Deliberacions

Cujus contrarium malum bonum, cujus bonum malum.

Non tenet in ijs rebus quarum vis in temperamento et mensurâ sita est.

Dum vitant stulti vitia in contraria currunt

× Media via nulla est quæ nec amicos parit nec inimicos tollit

Solons law that in states every man should declare him self of one faction. Neutralitye:

Vtinam esses calidus aut frigidus sed quoniam tepidus es eveniet vt te expuam ex ore meo.

Dixerunt fatui medium tenuere beatj

Cujus origo occasio bona, bonum; cujus mala malum.

Non tenet in ijs malis quæ vel mentem informant, vel affectum corrigunt, siue resipiscentiam inducendo siue necessitatem, nec etiam in fortuitis.

No man gathereth grapes of thornes nor figges of thistelles

The nature of every thing is best consydered in the seed

Primum mobile turnes about all y[e]. rest of y[e]. Orbes.

A good or yll foundacion.

× Ex malis moribus bonæ leges.

παθηματα μαθηματα.

When thinges are at the periode of yll they turn agayne

Folio 128, front—continued.

Many effectes like the serpent that deuoureth her moother so they destroy their first cause as inopia luxuria etc.

The fashion of D. Hert. to the dames of Lond. Your way is to be sicker

Usque adeo latet vtilitas

Aliquisque malo fuit vsus in illo

Folio 128, back.

Quod ad bonum finem dirigitur bonum, quod ad mulum malum

Folio 129, front.

[Blank]

Folio 129, back.

Philologia

colors of good and euill

Folio 130, front.

Some choice Frensh Proverbes.

Il a chié en son chapeau et puis s'en va couvert
Par trop debatre la verité se perd.
Apres besogne fait le fou barguine.
L'hoste et le poisson passes trois jours puent.
Le mort n'ha point d'amis, Le malade et l'absent qu'vn demye.
Il est tost trompé qui mal ne pense.
La farine du diable s'en va moitie en son.
Qui prest a l'ami, perd au double.
C'est vn valett du diable, qui fait plus qu'on luy command.
Il n'est horologe plus iust que le ventre.
Mere pitieuse, fille rigueuse
Il commence bien a mourrir qui abandonne son desir.
Chien qui abaye de loin ne mord pas.
Achete maison faite, femme a faire
Le riche disne quand il veut, le poure quand il peut.
Bien part de sa place qui son amy y lesse.
Il n'y a melieur mirroir que le vieil amy.
Amour fait beaucoup, mais l'argent fait tout.
L'amour la tousse et la galle ne se peuvent celer.
Amour fait rage, mais l'argent fait marriage.
Ma chemise blanche, baise mon cul tous les dimanches.
Mieux vaut vn tenes, que deux fois l'aurez.
Craindre ce qu'on peut vaincre, est vn bas courage.
A folle demande il ne faut point de responce.

Folio 130, front—continued.

Qui manie ses propres affaires, ne souille point se mains.

Argent receu les bras rompus.

Vn amoreux fait touiours quelque chose folastre.

Le povre qui donne au riche demande

Six heures dort l'escholier, sept ye voyager, huict ye vigneron, et neuf en demand le poltron.

La guerre fait les larrons et la paix les meine au gibbett

Au prester couzin germaine, au rendre fils de putaine

Qui n'ha point du miel en sa cruche, qu'il en aye en sa bouche.

Langage de Hauts bonnetts.

Les paroles du soir ne sembles a celles du matin.

Qui a bon voisin a bon matin.

Estre en la paille jusque au ventre.

Il faut prendre le temps comme il est, et les gens comme ils sont.

Il n'est Tresor que de vivre a son aise.

La langue n'a point d'os, et casse poitrine et dos.

Quand la fille pese vn auque, ou luy peut mettre la coque.

Il en tuera dix de la chandelle, et vingt du chandelier.

Folio 130, back.

Qui seme de Chardons recuielle des espines

Il n'est chassé que de vieux levriers.

Qui trop se haste en beau chemin se fourvoye.

Il ne choisit pas qui emprunt.

Ostez vn vilain au gibett, il vous y mettra.

Son habit feroit peur au voleur.

J'employerai verd et sec.

Tost attrappé est le souris, qui n'a pour tout qu'vn pertuis.

Le froid est si apre, qu'il me fait battre le tambour avec les dents.

Homme de deux visages, n'aggree en ville ny en villages.

Perdre la volee pour le bound.

Homme roux et femme barbue de cinquante pas les salüe.

Quand beau vient sur beau il perd sa beauté.

Les biens de la fortune passe comme la lune.

Ville qui parle, femme qui escoute, l'vne se prend, lautre se foute.

Coudre le peau du renard, à celle du lyon.

Il a la conscience large comme la manche d'vn cordelier.

Brusler la chandelle par les deux bouts.

Bon bastard c'est d'avanture, meschant c'est la nature.

Argent content portent medecine.

Bonne renommee vaut plus que cincture dorée.

Folio 130, back—continued.

Fille qui prend, se vend; fille qui donne s'abbandonne.

Fais ce que tu dois, avien que pourra.

Il est tost deceu qui mal ne pense.

Vos finesses sont cousües de fil blanc, elles sont trop apparentes.

Assez demand qui se plaint.

Assez demand qui bien sert.

Il ne demeure pas trop qui vient a la fin.

Secrett de dieux, secrett de dieux

Ton fils repeu et mal vestu, ta fille vestue et mal repue.

Du dire au fait il y a vn grand trait.

Courtesye tardive est discourtesye.

Femme se plaint, femme se deult, femme est malade quand elle veut—

Et par Madame S^{te}. Marie, quand elle veut, elle est guerrye.

Quie est loin du plat, est prez de son dommage.

Le Diable estoit alors en son grammaire.

Il a vn quartier de la lune en sa teste.

Homme de paille vaut vne femme d'or.

Amour de femme, feu d'estoupe.

Fille brunette gaye et nette

Renard qui dort la mattinée, n'a pas la langue emplumée.

Folio 131, front.

Tout est perdu qu'on donne au fol.

Bonnes paroles n'escorche pas la langue.

Pour durer il faut endurer

Qui veut prendre vn oiseau, qu'il ne l'effarouche.

Soleil qui luise au matin, femme qui parle latin, enfant nourri du vin ne vient point a bonne fin.

Il peut hardiment heurter a la porte, qui bonnes novelles apporte.

A bon entendeur ne faut que demy mot.

Qui fol envoye fol attend.

La faim chaisse le loup hors du bois.

Qui peu se prize, Dieu l'advise.

En pont, en planche, en riviere, valett devant, maistre arriere.

L'oeil du maistre engraisse le chevall.

Qui mal entend, mal respond.

Mal pense qui ne repense.

Mal fait qui ne pairfait.

Si tous les fols portoient marrottes, on ne sçauroit pas de quell bois se chaufer

Mieux vaut en paix vn oeuf, qu'en guerre vn boeuf.

Couper l'herbe sous les pieds.

Toutes les heures ne sont pas meures.

Qui vit a compte, vit a honte.

Meschante parole jettée, va par toute alla volée.

Amour se nourrit de ieune chaire

Innocence porte avec soy sa deffence.

Il ne regard plus loin que le bout de son nez.

A paroles lourdes, aureilles sourdes.

Folio 131, front—continued.

Ce n'est pas Evangile, qu'on dit parmi la ville.

Qui n'a patience n'a rien.

De mauvais payeur, foin ou paille

En fin les renards se troue chez le pelletier.

Qui prest a l'ami perd au double

Chantez a l'asne il vous fera de petz

Mieux vault glisser du pied, que de la langue.

Tout vient a point a chi peut attendre.

Il n'est pas si fol qu'il en porte l'habit.

Il est plus fol, qui a fol sens demand.

Nul n'a trop de sens, n'y d'argent.

En seurté dort qui n'a que perdre.

Le trou trop overt sous le nez fait porter soulier dechirez.

A laver la teste d'vn Asne, on ne perd que le temps et la lexive.

Chi choppe et ne tombe pas adiouste a ces pas.

Folio 131, back.

Amour, toux et fumée, en secrett ne sont demeurée.

Il a pour chaque trou vne cheville.

Il n'est vie que d'estre content.

Si tu veux cognoistre villain, baille luy la baggette en main.

Le boeuf salé, fait trover le vin sans chandelle.

Le sage va toujours la sonde a la main.

Qui se couche avec les chiens, se leve avec de puces.

A tous oiseaux leur nids sont beaux

Ovrage de commune, ovrage de nul.

Oy, voi, et te tais, si tu veux vivre en paix.

Rouge visage et grosse panche, ne sont signes de penitence.

A celuy qui a son paste au four, on peut donner de son tourteau.

Au serviteur le morceau d'honneur.

Pierre qui se remüe n'accuille point de mousse

Necessité fait trotter la vieille.

Nourriture passe nature.

La mort n'espargne ny Roy ny Roc.

En mangeant l' appetit vient.

Table sans sel, bouche sans salive

Les maladyes vient a cheval, et s'en returne a pieds.

Tenez chauds le pied et la teste, au demeurant vivez en beste.

Faillir est vne chose humaine, se repentir divine, perseverer diabolique.

Fourmage est sain qui vient de ciche main.

Folio 131, back—continued.

Si tu veux engraisser promptement, mangez avec faim, bois a loisir et lentement.

A l'an soixante et douse, temps est qu'on se house.

Vin sur laict c'est souhait, lait sur vin c'est venin

Faim fait disner passetemps souper.

Le maux terminans en ique, font au medecine la nique.

Au morceau restiffe esperon de vin.

Vn oeuf n'est rien, deux font grand bien, trois c'est assez, quattre c'est fort, cinque c'est la mort.

Apres les poire le vin ou le prestre

Qui a la santé est riche et ne le scait pas.

A la trogne on cognoist l'yvrogne.

Le fouriere de la lune a marque le logis.

Vne pillule fromentine, vne dragme sermentine, et la balbe[1] d'vne galline est vne bonne medecine.

Il faut plus tost prendre garde avec qui tu bois et mange, qu'a ce que tu bois et mange.

Qui tout mange le soir, le lendemain rogne son pain noir

Vin vieux, amy vieux, et or vieux sont amez en tous lieux.

NOTE.—[1] "balbe" may be read "balle."

Folio 132, front.

Qui veut vivre sain, disne peu et soupe moins.

Lever a six, manger a dix, souper a six, coucher a dix, font l'homme vivre dix fois dix.

De tous poissons fors que la tenche, prenez les dos, lessez le ventre.

Qui couche avec la soif, se leve avec la santé.

Amour de garze et saut de chien, ne dure si l'on ne dit tien.

Il en est plus assotté qu'vn fol de sa marotte.

Qui fol envoye fol attende.

Pennache de boeuf.

Vn Espagnol sans Jesuite est comme perdis sans orange.

C'est la maison de Robin de la vallée, ou il y a ny pott au feu, ny escuelle lavée.

Celuy gouverne bien mal le miel qui n'en taste.

Auiourdhuy facteur, demaine fracteur.

Il est crotte en Archidiacre.

Apres trois jours on s'ennuy, de femme, d'hoste, et de pluye.

Il n'est pas eschappé qui son lien traine.

En la terre des aveugles, le borgne est Roy.

Il faut que la faim soit bien grande, quand les loups mange l'vn l'autre.

Il n'est[1] faut qu'vne mouche luy passe, par devant le nez, pour le facher.

La femme est bien malade, quand elle ne se peut tenir sur le dos.

NOTE.—For [1] "Il n'est faut" may be read "Il n'en faut."

Folio 132, front—continued.

Il n'a pas bien assise ses lunettes.
Cette flesche n'est pas sorti de son carquois.
L'affaire vas a quattre roües
Merchand d'allumettes
C'est vn marchand qui prend l'argent sans conter ou peser.
Je vous payeray en monnoye de cordelier.
Vous avez mis le doit dessus.
S'embarquer sans bisquit.
Coucher a l'enseigne de l'estoile
On n'y trove ny tric ny troc.
Cecy n'est pas de mon gibier.
Joyeux comme sourris en graine
Il a beaucoup de grillons en la teste.
Elle a son Çardinall
Il est fourni du fil et d'esguille.
Chevalier de Corneuaille.
Angleterre le Paradis de femmes, le pourgatoire de valetts, l'enfer de chevaux.
Le mal An entre en nageant.
Qui a la fievre au Mois de May, le rest de l'an vit sain et gay.
Fol a vint cinque carrattes
Celuy a bon gage du Chatte qui en tient la peau.
Il entend autant comme truye en espices
Nul soulas humaine sans helas
In (*sic*) n'est pas en seureté qui ne mescheut onques.

Folio 133, front.

[Blank]

Folio 133, back.

Some choice Frensh Prover[bs.]

FROM
SPENSER'S "FAERIE QUEEN," 1617.

THE · DE VINNE PRESS
IMPRIMATUR